I'm a Choir Director??!

I'M A CHOIR DIRECTOR??!

REHEARSING EVEN THE ROWDIEST VOLUNTEER CHOIR AND LOVING EVERY MINUTE OF IT.

Publishing

JOEL PLAAG

Copyright © 2020 Joel F. Plaag
All rights reserved.

Excerpt of "In the Beginning," by Aaron Copland used with permission of Boosey&Hawkes. Excerpt of "Dorian Dance," by Michael Joy used with permission of Jeffers Handbell Supply. Excerpt of "Magnificat" by Jonathan Willcocks used with permission of Lorenz publications.

First paperback edition: June, 2020

978-0-578-67877-1 (paperback)
978-0-578-67878-8 (e-book)

Poogie the Pup Publishing
www.joelplaag.cc

Table of Contents

PART ONE: BECOMING A CHOIR DIRECTOR 1

CHAPTER 1 IN FRONT OF THE CHOIR 2
    Conclusion 7

CHAPTER 2 WHY WE SING... 8
    Reasons why we sing 9
    To fulfill a need 13
    Conclusion 16

CHAPTER 3 THE MUSICAL CONNECTION 18
    Preparing the music 19
    Recordings: When do we use them? 23
    Conclusion 24

PART TWO: THE MECHANICS OF CONCUCTING 25

CHAPTER 4 THE PATTERNS 26
Choral conducting versus instrumental conducting 27
The patterns of conducting 28
What is an ictus? 29
The beat patterns 29
Other Patterns 32
What to remember: 33
Conclusion 34

CHAPTER 5 CONDUCTING DIFFERENT METERS 35
Changing the meter 35
Marking beat patterns 39
Conclusion 48

CHAPTER 6 PREPARATION 49
When to use a preparatory beat 50
Conclusion 55

CHAPTER 7 THE LEFT HAND 57
Resting position 58
Cues 59
Use of the eyes 60
Types of cues 62
Cut-offs 65
The gesture of syncopation 68
Combining gestures of syncopation and other motions 70
Conclusion 73

CHAPTER 8 THE BATON 74
The meaning of the baton 75
Choosing the baton 76
Holding the baton 80

PART ONE: Becoming a Choir Director

    Conclusion 82

  CHAPTER 9 STOPS AND STARTS 83
    The fermata.. 85
    Recitative.. 89
    Common recitative solutions 90
    Conclusion 94

PART THREE: PREPARING FOR REHEARSAL 95

  CHAPTER 10 BEFORE THE FIRST REHEARSAL..................... 96
    Space.. 97
    Order 99
    Connections 101
    Musical ideas (how to prepare for rehearsal) 104
    Conclusion 107

  CHAPTER 11 APPROACHING A NEW SCORE 109
    Conclusion 123

  CHAPTER 12 DEVELOPING THE REHEARSAL PLAN 125
    Getting ready for the concert 134
    Conclusion 136

PART FOUR: THE REHEARSAL......................138

  CHAPTER 13 THE WARM-UP.. 139
    Pause – the mental warm-up 140
    The vocal warm-up process 144
    Conclusion 147

  CHAPTER 14 IN THE REHEARSAL 148
    The warm-up.. 149
    The rehearsal 149
    Rehearsing together.. 152
    The end of rehearsal 155
    After rehearsal... 156
    Conclusion 157

In Front of the Choir

PART FIVE: THE REST OF THE STORY 158

CHAPTER 15   WHAT ELSE DO WE DO? 159
Not just conducting 161
Other tools for the choir director 163
For those whose calling is in the church 164
Conclusion 168

CHAPTER 16   IF YOU BUILD IT… 170
When they are missing 172
Letters to the Choir 173
Setting Expectations 178
Conclusion 180

CHAPTER 17   CODA 182

FURTHER READING 187
ACKNOWLEDGEMENTS 188
ABOUT THE AUTHOR 192

PART ONE:

Becoming a Choir Director

Chapter 1

In Front of the Choir

It looks so easy – wave the hands, the music flows. The mental, logistical and physical demands quietly work in the background.

No one ever said conducting the choir was easy.

For most choir directors, filling our choirs with volunteers is an especially tough job. We get to work with wonderful voices, varying personalities, and non-musical issues just as much as making music. We have people who come to

PART ONE: Becoming a Choir Director

rehearsal excited, sad, angry, thrilled, and glad to be out of the house. Sometimes we have people that don't show up at all. When they do, it's magical.

Music is a calling – so many of us are moved to work in schools, in the community, as professional musicians, and in churches. It requires us to study and learn as much as we can about music and the art of music. A volunteer director requires a special calling though – whether religious, musical, or simply caring about one's church or synagogue. We all come into this field in various and surprising ways.

As a new conductor, I took over for a volunteer who could play the piano, was extremely nice, loved the church, and wanted to make a difference. My accompanist was a fantastic pianist. For me, it was heaven – it was what I had longed to do! Though my motivation was strong, my choir may not have held the same excitement in my rehearsals. Nonetheless, they felt the call to sing. Years later, I watch countless directors – professionals, amateurs, and novices – who have this same motivation: the need to work with a choir.

When I started working as a church choir director, I had little idea of what I was doing. I knew that I wanted to conduct. I knew I had the knowledge in there *somewhere,* but I wasn't sure where to begin. New music sat in front of me. Fear gripped my every approach. I was still years away from any sort of spiritual connection. In my mind I knew that if these people knew I was a fraud like I thought I was, they wouldn't have been so eager to hire me.

Many reading this might identify – loving the idea of being a conductor but maybe not able to quite make it happen. Maybe you play the piano and direct the church choir or community chorus because there was no one else. If you're new to choirs, or new-at-heart to choirs, this book is for you.

Part of the reason I wanted to write this was to clarify my own work, share some of my experiences and tricks so that you do not have to make some of the same mistakes. This book is divided into five sections. You can read them in sequence or go directly to the chapter that seems most applicable.

My career path has twisted, turned, and changed dramatically. After that first church choir, I was sure I needed to work as a professor – an academic – and I worked extremely hard to become a good professor. Later, after getting my first taste of church choir and community chorus, I heard a new call to work volunteers.

PART ONE: Becoming a Choir Director

So, you want to be a choir director? Volunteer choir directors get the good and the bad singers, but first and foremost, we get wonderful people. In the choir are many personalities, and miraculously, we get to lead them.

What does it mean to conduct a choir? *Conducting is an act of internal acceptance*. We change what we can with each of our groups, and we accept when we can't. We work at changing those gestures and ideas in ourselves to make sure the choir can follow us. We grieve and learn from the times that our gestures are inadequate, that our performances were less than, and our results fell short of what we wanted.

Together, we will go through the road of becoming a choir director. Church and synagogue choir directors have a sacred and challenging part of worship, needing the utmost care and sensitivity. Community chorus directors have an important outlet for people near them. In our discussion, we will talk about conducting and its beautiful, nuanced gestures. We will talk about music preparation. We will talk about the rehearsal process. Throughout it all, we will talk about how choral music brings us closer to God.

We all come from different faith backgrounds, and because of that, we will try to be universal in the spiritual. Feel free to use prayer –

even something so simple as *'help me'* - to assist with your musical journey. Your own prayer will be more than enough to form that connection and touch your singers. With God's help, we will all become better conductors.

I will never forget seeing my father in the parking lot after one of my required conducting recitals for school. He was not a musician and often said how he really was unfamiliar with classical music, but he loved to come to my concerts. He was my biggest fan. One night though, in a dark, foreboding parking lot, I saw my dad after a concert. The concert had gone horribly. My cues were unsure, notes were wrong, and the love that I had for the art of choral music was a distant memory. As I stood angry at my lack of ability, I stared into my father's face, he looked at me with those eyes – he could sometimes see right through me - and I think he knew what I was thinking.

"That was awful," I said, full of rage and fury at myself. If I could have pulled my soul out and beat it with my fists, I would have done so. Yet my father, who never understood my emotions or the constant, self-inflicted rages, said nothing. He just looked at my rather overdramatic frame. "You'll do better next time." That was it.

Three years later, Dad was again sitting front-and-center during the first time I conducted

PART ONE: Becoming a Choir Director

Franz Joseph Haydn's (1732-1809) *Lord Nelson Mass* with a community chorus that I had put together by writing letters to local church choir directors. It worked! It only took a little patience.

Dad looked the same after that performance. He was proud of me for both – the failure, and the success. In Dad's eyes, I was his son, 'the conductor.' If I was able to get all the cues or not in whatever-the-piece-was-that-I-messed-up back in school, or if the choir was perfect in that night's concert, it didn't matter. What mattered was that I was up there, in front of people, doing what I did and enjoying myself.

Conclusion

Though it would take a few more years for this lesson to sink in, the lesson is this:

There are people in the world who believe in you, in what you do, and your work. Stay close to those people, listen to them, and ignore the rest.

In today's judgmental world, this rule reigns supreme: be your own judge, and never take yourself too seriously.

Chapter 2

Why We Sing

A few years ago, I went to a conference of the Association of Disciples Musicians. (I work in a Disciples of Christ Church.) Not knowing anyone, I was rather apprehensive about attending this conference. Despite the profession I have chosen, I am shy and somewhat introverted around new people. Being new, I felt out of place and out of my element.

I envy people who can walk into a situation not knowing anyone and feel right at home – I do

PART ONE: Becoming a Choir Director

not have that gift. I moved from workshop to workshop, sitting in the back, near the exit, speaking to no one. Yet each morning was rehearsal for the Chapel Choir, and as a newcomer, singing in it seemed like the thing to do. I sat down with a room full of strangers and sang my part. I sat in my row and others, to my chagrin, sat down next to me. I discussed intervals and splitting parts with the other basses. I looked at my notes. During moments when the director was working with others, I studied the difficult sections.

In a span of just a few minutes of rehearsal the magic happened again. I belonged. I had a place. Right there, among these random people whose names I knew only from the badges on their lanyards, I had a place.

I learned that singing binds us together in very intimate and immediate ways.

Reasons why we sing

1. We sing for a sense of belongingness.

Nothing says, "I am supposed to be here," like singing the same words at the same time next to a lot of other people. No other feeling comes close to it. It is a level of intimacy that is hard to reproduce. Imagine if each of us knew our voice part all the time, and that in random places (I write this in the era of social distancing) we all sang the same thing with correct notes at once.

2. *We sing because it uses our bodies.*

My instrumentalist friends are always laughing because singers – especially choral singers – are loud, demonstrative and even a little rambunctious. Singing, unlike playing piano or many other instruments, uses our bodies as well as our minds and spirits. Because it uses our *bodies* solely, we are sensitive about our sounds. How often have we come across people who say "oh I can't sing," and then accidentally sing well when no one is watching. We never want to be told we are terrible singers, because it is a critique on ourselves.

3. *We sing because we are moved by the words.*

Music *and* words. What a combination! In the orchestra, program music can only imply story. Singers use poetry, words, scripture and other texts that wind up staying in our minds forever. I remember hearing a famous choir director say this: "I did not learn Bible verses because I was a great Sunday school student! I knew them because I *rehearsed* those words!" Congregants rarely come out of services quoting the sermon – they come out singing the melody!

PART ONE: Becoming a Choir Director

Pastors want the words of the anthems and hymns to match their sermons' messages, but sometimes our good music is sacrificed to inferior hymns because of the words. This is a disservice, both to message and to music, and happens when the pastor looks at the musician as employee instead of collaborator. The memorable – or forgettable – quality of music can sabotage even the best sermon.

4. *We sing to create harmony.*

Harmony, whether implied through monophonic (one line) singing, or directly by two or more parts singing notes that agree or disagree with each other, is one of the greatest experiences. Who does not want to hear an *a cappella* final chord sung so perfectly in tune, so resonant, that the notes seem to have a life of their own? Which is more exciting: everyone singing in unison, or everyone on their own part, working together to create something larger?

5. *We sing to encounter God.*

There is a reason that we can be moved by the words that are sung; a reason people feel something when they sing. We experience one of the greatest gifts available in our natural world – musical harmony. Music moves us to experience God in ways that spoken word cannot.

Why We Sing

A long time ago, I was given this poem:

Why We Teach Music

Not because we expect you to major in music.
Not because we expect you to play or sing all your life.
Not so you can relax.
Not so you can have fun.

But
So you will be human.
So you will recognize beauty.
So you will be sensitive.
So you will be closer to an infinite beyond this world.
So you will have something to cling to.
So you will have more love, more compassion, more gentleness, more good -
In short, more life.

Of what value will it be to make a prosperous living unless you know how to live?

That is why we teach music.

-Author Unknown

6. We sing to Praise God.

PART ONE: Becoming a Choir Director

As choral singers, we find that we live for the harmonics – harmonics that come from a nature system that we had absolutely no part in creating. Because we had no part in making the background structure of music, we marvel at the majesty of the music that we get to make. We remember that there must be a loving God who must have designed all of this.

7. *We sing to serve.*

Despite what some may think, the people we see every week do not always join the choir because they are the best singers, best sight-readers, or have some great knowledge or insight into music. *Most volunteer choirs sing in order to be of service. They remain in choir because they feel like they are making a positive contribution.* Singers sing because they may not be good organizers, church potluck bakers, guitar players, or Sunday school teachers, but they can raise their voices when the notes go up and lower their voices when the notes go down. Neither good or bad directors stop choir members from coming, because singers feel like their presence is needed every week to make a difference in their worship service or community.

To fulfill a need

It is important to know why our singers are there. For years, I thought they were there because

I had some great, wonderful things to teach them. I really thought (I am embarrassed to admit this) that the volunteer choirs were there --- for me!

Now I know. Singers are there because of singing; because of the music they get to do. Not because of me. Not much, anyway.

On a night in my first church choir, we were rehearsing a two-part arrangement of *Come Thou Fount*. We rehearsed the same spot over and over and over again. I was sure that the bass constantly missing the notes would *eventually* figure it out if we kept working at it. So I would stop, and correct, and stop, and correct. Finally, one of the tenors, a 93-year-old man and father of the former director, yells out from the back row:

"WHY DON'T YOU JUST LET US SING!!!!!!"

I was flustered. I stammered through some grand explanation as to why we needed to sing in parts. It was something grandiose to the effect that the world was a much better place if only the basses would sing the harmony and not the melody two octaves down. I stewed about that man who so unfairly disrupted my wonderful rehearsal. Later, in hindsight I realized he was right. I failed to comprehend one of the elementary parts of choir – people want to sing. They want to rehearse, and they want to get better, but they do not want me to

PART ONE: Becoming a Choir Director

show how they are wrong. Most times, they already know.

In the past, conductors dictated their will to the orchestra. Toscanini, Mahler, Wagner, even Beethoven were all considered tyrants on the podium, probably as much out of an abundance of ego as a desire to have the music performed perfectly. Now, conductors must be focused, driven and soft-spoken. They show the sound and technique they want because they have studied the score. They convey through inspiration, rather than humiliation.

When I started my career, I read a veteran church choir director's book suggesting utmost discipline and order in the choir rehearsal. If a singer came in late, the conductor should ask "why?" If a singer dared make a joke about the conductor or about the music, he or she should be disciplined. Nothing else should be tolerated, the author said. Today the rules have changed. Singers come to our rehearsals after work, sitting for two hours each day in traffic. They come amidst a hurried schedule between picking kids up from school, grandchildren's dance recitals, and watching after-school sports. Singers come after taking care of a convalescing spouse, raising grandkids and after a full day of caring for children who are ill. We must not assume that the volunteer singer will come just because of good music. People come to rehearsal to feel healing and belonging, and we have a higher calling today to provide those things first.

In this book, we will explore the basics and the nuances of conducting a volunteer choir. We will learn about movement, the inner ear, creating phrases, the technical gesture, preparation, and how to tighten the rehearsal process. It is my hope that through the course of this book you will become a better conductor than I was. In some ways, this book is about making amends to the many people that I conducted in my early career, when I lacked the gestural language or the rehearsal chops to say what needed to be said. It is an amends for when I missed patience in the rehearsal room or when nit-picking to perfection meant more than the exuberance of performance.

Conclusion

It is my hope that you will come away with a better understanding of what choir directors do, and how to be the best choir director possible. It is also my hope that you will walk away from here with the idea that maybe, many of the problems that we face in conducting are *internal* rather than *external*. Our gestures or knowledge of the music, our expectation of the ensemble, our tempo, and

PART ONE: Becoming a Choir Director

our own insecurity may be what hampers our ensemble the most.

Finally, I encourage you to pray for guidance to direct others. If God is truly the Source of all of this, creator of music and from whom all things are made, God's strength will support you in leading a group of singers, no matter what your perceived faults.

There are a few qualifications needed to fully use this book. First, you must be a musician of some sort. Conductors must be able to read and understand the music on the page. This includes pianists, guitarists, singers, flute players, oboists, string players and percussionists. I have seen all these types of musicians become successful choir directors. Second, you must have the need or desire to learn more, because an empty canvas makes for the best painting. Third, you must be courageous – to stand in front of a choir, to lead others, is the very definition of courage. Finally, if that courage seems missing, find a Higher Power – a God whom you can believe in. Whatever your religious affinity, find an accepting and loving creator – and ask for guidance.

Chapter 3

The Musical Connection

Before we begin our first rehearsal and the excitement of working with the ensemble, we need to do some inside work by ourselves, for conducting and rehearsing start with our own vision of the music. What is that vision? How do we communicate it? Pianists can play through the piece. Singers perform each of the lines, listen to a recording, or play the parts together with some semblance of accompaniment. We analyze, listen, interpret, and decide how fast,

PART ONE: Becoming a Choir Director

how loud, how articulate, or how many breaths we take, but how do we show it?

The eyes may be windows to the soul, but the hands are the bread and butter of the conductor. Even though it makes more sense to use our dominant hand to conduct, whatever that may be, conductors *always use the right hand.* For lefties, I sympathize how difficult it is to learn with the right hand, but fear not, when the time is right, you will be able to use both hands with the nimbleness and dexterity that our right-handed colleagues can only dream about.

Here is a five-step method I use to approach a new piece of music for choir rehearsals:

Preparing the music

1. Become acquainted with the music.

Spend some time alone with the music. Your initial read of a piece of music when you are choosing it to program into a concert or service may be the first time you see it. Play through the parts – as many as you can at once. If you are an adept pianist, playing open score should present few problems. If you are not a great pianist, play through two parts at a time. Start with Soprano and Alto. Then play Tenor and Bass. Finally, play through the accompaniment as best you can. Answer the following questions in your head:

The Musical Connection

- What is the harmonic structure?
- Does anything recur?
- Are there any unusual chords?
- Are there any unusual jumps, especially on a page turn?
- What is the text like? What mood does it evoke?
- Are there any spots where the choir does not sing together? (This is called *counterpoint* and presents additional challenges both for you as director and for the ensemble. The easiest way to describe counterpoint is a place where the words do not line up.)
- Be aware of any time or meter changes. I like to mark them with green highlighter.
- Do you love the music? (If you don't love it, don't program it!)

2. Study the score.

Play through the piano part again (if there is one) to get a sense of the harmonic structure of the piece and how it flows. Look at the time signatures, the dynamics, and any speed changes.

After playing through the accompaniment, do so again while singing the soprano part. Alternatively, sing through one of the lower parts (alto, tenor, or bass) while playing the accompaniment or the soprano part. If you wish to use a simplified version of the accompaniment, (i.e.

PART ONE: Becoming a Choir Director

omit fast runs or playing only the outer notes of the treble and bass lines) do so. The goal is to get a sense of the line.

Pay attention to:
- Entrances that occur in a single part by themselves (such as a solo entrance, or in counterpoint).
- Initial entrances and finding the first notes of phrases.
- Fast or difficult rhythms, or sections where a lot of words are said quickly. Practice these by yourself (undoubtedly, you will be teaching them later!)
- Changes in dynamics - especially sudden, dramatic changes.
- Changes in speed or meter.

3. Identify cues.

Choirs love cues! It gives them a sense of comfort to know we are right there with them, ready to help. Cues can be highlighted on each part in yellow and should be given for:
- Initial entrances.
- Individual part entrances.
- Words or phrases that begin off a beat.
- At the beginning of an important melody.
- A change of dynamics or speed.

4. Step away from the piano.

This is the way I find that I really, really know a piece: can I sing it, out loud, with no accompaniment? Can I sing through the melody that begins in the accompaniment and follow it into each voice part? Can I demonstrate all the cues? Most importantly, can I change parts?

This is the step which indicates whether the piece is ready to be taught: jump voice parts from one to another without having to get the first note of the piano. If you cannot do this, sit at the piano and find the missing note(s). Then practice doing the same thing away from the piano. If you can sing it, you know it. If not, keep working!

5. Practice.

Now that you are an expert in the music, practice conducting it. Most importantly, try to cue places where different notes or instruments enter. Sing along with your movements.

Finally, practice so that you will look out from your score. If the choir knows their parts, they will appear confident (and of course be saying the words at the right time!). If they are unsure, they will look down. This visual cue will be helpful in determining if the choir is comfortable with individual parts. If you are looking down, you'll miss the choir's visual cue. (Some think that I am looking directly at them!)

PART ONE: Becoming a Choir Director

When I was learning how to direct a choir, learning the music was the biggest *mystery* to me. There are several different schools of thought at how to internalize a score. Some said, "play and sing," where one part was played while the other was sung. Some said "sing through each part by itself – instrumental and vocal." Some said "play everything at the piano at once." For different people, there may be different ways of learning a piece of music. In my experience, these five steps outlined above *always* work. Most of the time, if the choir seems baffled in learning the music, or is not performing it well, it is because I do not know it well enough. I have work to do on my own, away from the choir. Remember: *conducting is an act of internal acceptance.*

Recordings: When do we use them?

As a graduate student, I had to learn new pieces and be ready to conduct them on a moment's notice often quickly. Today, with the advent of YouTube, recordings of just about any piece are available. Recordings help conductors have an idea how the piece should sound and can be used in emergencies when a piece needs to be learned and taught quickly. *It does not replace the need for real, honest, thorough score study.* Yes, during beginning rehearsals when teaching notes or determining tempos, recordings can be extremely helpful in a pinch, but they will not help form a vision of the music. They also will not help practice how to conduct, as recordings do not react to gestures.

Conclusion

As I began my musical career, my piano chops were less than stellar. However, the five-part method described earlier was helpful and came about after hard-learned experience. As the years have progressed, so have my piano skills, but I still rely on this system. Sometimes, if I choose a piece that I can play at sight, I am at a disadvantage because I am tempted to skip singing through parts *a cappella.* I wind up having to go back and review one or more steps to internalize the score because the choir has not mastered the piece well.

PART TWO:

The Mechanics of Conducting

Chapter 4

The Patterns

If you have sung in a choir all your life, you are familiar with the conducting patterns. You may even already know that patterns are a must for instrumentalists so they can count measures and know exactly where to play. Many do not realize how important the patterns are for singers – especially when the time signatures change often. They are a necessary part of the conducting process. In many conducting books, a great deal of writing is devoted to the patterns, yet I have never heard anyone come out of a concert saying, "Wasn't Maestro's 5/8 pattern AMAZING?!?"

The pattern is the unsung hero of conducting. It keeps singers together all through the piece. Without it, there is no modicum of communication between leader and ensemble. Mastery of this through drill is *essential* because expressive music making and conducting cannot happen without the basic elements of the language.

Choral conducting versus instrumental conducting

Choral conducting usually requires breathing, unlike conducting percussion ensembles (such as handbells). There are gestures that can be made for choirs that cannot with orchestras, and vice-versa. However, in most cases, *conducting is conducting is conducting* – the mechanics are the same. Whether in front of a band, orchestra, choir, jazz combo, or fourth-grade recorder choir, the fundamentals of conducting are *identical.* The music, not the ensemble, dictates everything else. I have found that those who relegate themselves to one "type" of conducting are missing out on a vast repertoire, and may miss the opportunity to be good, clear conductors. For our instrumental friends, how can one understand an orchestral suite by Johann Sebastian Bach (1685-1750) if he has not conducted one of his cantatas? How can someone conduct The *Requiem* of Wolfgang Amadeus Mozart (1756-1791) if they haven't applied the same work to the overture to his opera *The Magic Flute*? Singers and instrumentalists alike will praise you for good, clear gesture that is not muddied by insistence of sticking to one type of ensemble. Division does not apply here; since there are many different types of music for us to conduct.

The patterns of conducting

Conducting uses four main patterns: ONE, TWO, THREE, or FOUR. I will use capital words to designate these patterns. These must be executed using the right hand – which can be tough at first for those of us that are lefties! (However, if you are a lefty and are having difficulty, try mirroring the right hand with your left hand at first, and then removing the left hand once the right hand becomes comfortable.)

Balanced/Unbalanced patterns

Balanced and unbalanced patterns refer to the number of divisions in each beat of the pattern. For instance, in a TWO pattern, a balance means that both beat represents three smaller beats (such as 2/4 or 6/8). An unbalanced pattern has a mixture of two or three divisions, such as in the TWO

PART TWO: The Mechanics of Conducting

pattern each beat consisting of 2 divisions and then 3 divisions (such as a 5/8 meter).

What is an ictus?

The *ictus* is the point where a beat occurs. In conducting, it is an imaginary horizontal line located just below or right at the sternum. The ictus serves as both a reference point as the ensemble begins, and as the actual point where the beat happens. When conducting, the gesture should appear to bounce off this imaginary line, creating a rebound that moves toward the next beat point.

The black line represents the ictus on the body.

The beat patterns

The ONE pattern
- Comes down to the ictus
- Up to start again.

The Patterns

ONE :fast 2/4 and fast 3/4 or 3/8

The TWO pattern

- Comes down to the ictus
- Moves away from the body
- Comes back to the body near the ictus point of the first beat.
- Bounces Up to start again.

 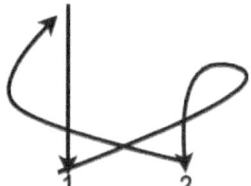

Balanced TWO: 2/4 and 6/8

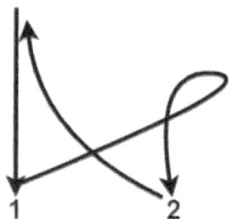 

Unbalanced TWO: 5/8 (2+3) and (3+2)

PART TWO: The Mechanics of Conducting

The THREE pattern

- Comes down to the ictus and moves *into* the body.
- Returns out away from the body to touch the ictus.
- After beat two, continues outward, and then returns in to touch the ictus again.
- After beat three, rebounds upward to startthe pattern again.

Balanced THREE: 3/4 and 9/8

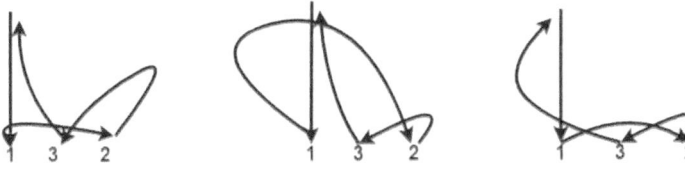

Unbalanced THREE: 7/8 (2+3+2), (3+2+2), and (2+2+3)

The FOUR pattern

- Comes down to the ictus for the first beat and rebounds *away* from the body.

- Moves back in to the body for beat two.
- After beat two rebounds in further (crossing the body) and returns outward to touch beat three.
- Rebounds away from the body and comes back inward to touch the ictus one more time in the center for beat four.
- Rebounds back up to where it started.

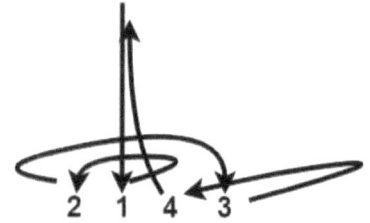

Balanced FOUR: 4/4

Balanced FOUR: 12/8

Other Patterns

A combination of smaller and larger beats and multiple touches to the ictus on each beat can create larger time signatures. Here is an example

PART TWO: The Mechanics of Conducting

of how to use the FOUR pattern to create a 10/8 measure of 2+2+3+3.

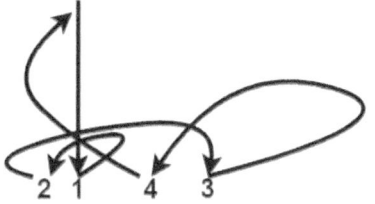

Unbalanced FOUR: 10/8 (2+2+3+3)

All other patterns are essentially based on these four. You can always touch each beat more than once to subdivide and therefore double the number of beats; a FOUR becomes EIGHT, and THREE becomes SIX.

What to remember:

1. THREE versus FOUR are easiest to confuse. Remember that in the THREE pattern, the rebound from beat one goes *into* the center of the body. In the FOUR pattern, the rebound for beat one goes *away* from the body.
2. Each of these patterns can be subdivided by touching the spot of each beat twice. This creates a six-beat pattern made up of a THREE (2+2+2), or an eight-beat pattern made up of a FOUR (2+2+2+2).
3. When subdividing, use more motion at the beginning of each large beat of the pattern.

The Patterns

For instance, in a SEVEN that is 3+2+2, use a larger rebound after beats three and five. This is both for the players/singers (so they know which beats to emphasize) and so you can keep track of where you are.

Conclusion

Like learning scales or key signatures, patterns are the basic vocabulary of the conductor. The power of these patterns cannot be understated. It may not earn you points from the audience but will certainly earn you points from your ensemble.

Chapter 5

Conducting Different Meters

C hanging meters is like stepping into a new pair of shoes. They look good but might lead to blisters.

Changing the meter

Meter changes are one of the most fun parts of conducting, and yet still require the most amount of practice. A good conductor can create these motions, but only after a *lot* of practice. Volunteer choirs sometimes change meters, but volunteer handbell choirs *always* change meters!

If you are new to conducting, you might be saying, "I'll never use this! I'll just pick pieces that stay in a single time signature." Not only does this limit what the choir can do, it also sets you as the conductor, on to a road of fear. Fear is never a helpful product in the rehearsal room and can lead to a smaller choir.

There are only two types of meter: duple – where the beat is divided into two – and triple – where the beat is divided into three. Patterns, and all music divides unceremoniously into one of these two groups.

This simple premise is the primary influence of our conducting patterns.

One of my favorite examples of the difference between duple and triple meter is the great masterwork by Giovanni Gabrieli (1557-1612), *In Ecclesiis.* At first hearing, I was struck at the dichotomy between the verses in duple meter, and the sudden shift to triple meter for the alleluias. Listening to as many recordings of this piece as I could find, I realized that some conductors keep the quarter note constant, so that the triple meter section moves slowly and introspectively.

I wasn't interested in that version. The second version, which I had experienced and heard

PART TWO: The Mechanics of Conducting

first, colored my perception of the relationship between the duple meter and triple meter sections. In this version, the half note speed remained the same through the transition to 3/4, and became a dotted half note at the same speed as the old half note, sending them skipping along to their whirling and thrilling conclusion. (After all, triple meter means joy!) Thanks to researching the manuscript, I know that either version is correct.

Giovanni Gabirieli. *In Ecclesiis.* Edited by Peter Rottländer. Distributed under the terms of the Choral Public Domain Library License (http://www.cpdl.org).

There are two ways to handle this tempo change:

1. Keep the quarter note the same.

Conducting Different Meters

- In 2/2, the quarter note is 124 beats per minute.
- In 3/4, the quarter note is also 124 beats per minute.
- The half note in 2/2 is faster than the dotted half note in 3/4.

2. Keep the half/dotted half note the same.
    - In 2/2, the quarter note is 124 beats per minute, or 62 half notes per minute.
    - In 3/4, the quarter note is 186 beats per minute, or 62 half notes per minute.
    - The half note in 2/2 is slower than the dotted half note in 3/4.

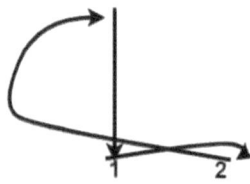

Creating the slower tempo change, as in example 1 above, means breaking the momentum

PART TWO: The Mechanics of Conducting

of the beat. Stop conducting while the ensemble continues singing and playing. When approaching the 3/4, create a preparatory beat in the new, slower tempo.

Stopping the pattern is an easy way to get the ensemble's attention and to change meters without having to create extra explanation. After all, good gesture is worth a thousand words!

Creating a tempo change to the faster speed means using an efficient, quick preparatory beat. Use a wider second beat as a preparation for the new, faster tempo.

Marking beat patterns

Now that we have discussed changing beats and beat patterns, it is important to notate the music so that we can quickly identify and conduct the correct pattern.

Meters can be tricky, especially when conducting instruments. It is important – imperative, really – to mark meters and conduct them correctly when they rapidly change, so they are not missed. Here are the markings I use for the patterns:

Conducting Different Meters

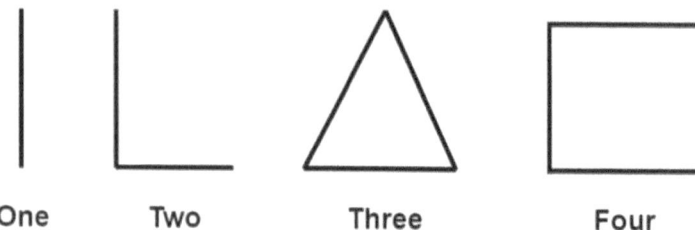

One   **Two**   **Three**   **Four**

Often, I will mark these shapes using highlighter in green directly on the score. If there are a multitude of tempo changes, I may mark these shapes on every measure. In addition, I can remind myself which beats to subdivide by placing a slash on each side of the shape to create five, six, seven or more beats. Each slash represents an additional touch on the same beat in the pattern. For example, to create a five, I use the TWO pattern with the downward beat touched twice, while the beat to the right gets touched three times before rebounding back to the top. On the shapes, move clockwise starting from the left, or you may choose any direction you wish, so long as it is consistent.

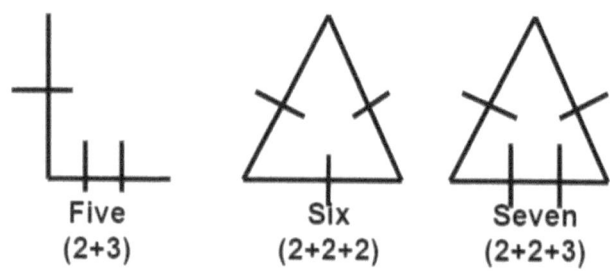

Five   **Six**   **Seven**
(2+3)   (2+2+2)   (2+2+3)

PART TWO: The Mechanics of Conducting

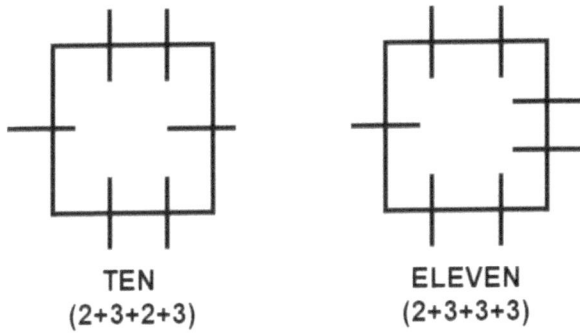

TEN
(2+3+2+3)

ELEVEN
(2+3+3+3)

In Aaron Copland's *In the Beginning*, not only does the number of beats change in each measure, but so do the groupings of twos and threes. To conduct this, we need to know what patterns the music created. Bracket the soloist's part using groups of two eighth notes and three eighth notes. The twos are marked by straight lines, the threes by arcs. Then determine the time signatures.

Conducting Different Meters

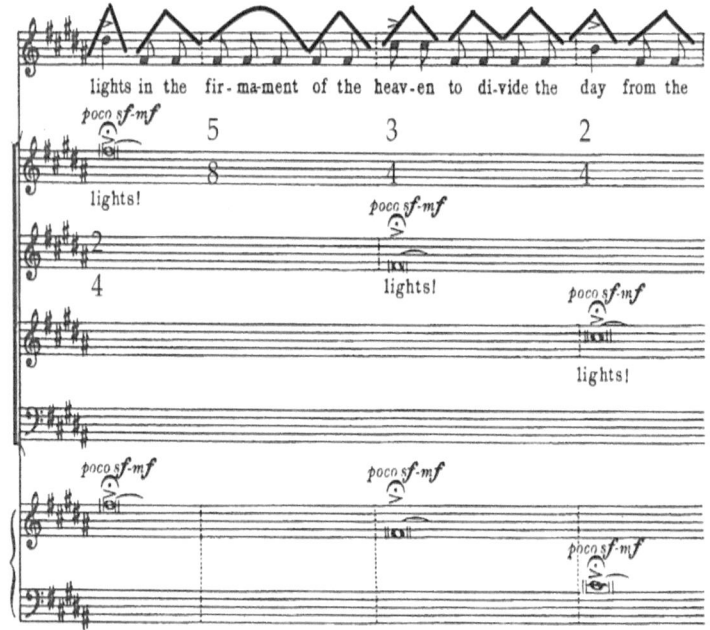

In the Beginning by Aaron Copland, © 1947 The Aaron Copland Fund For Music, Inc. Copyright Renewed. Boosey & Hawkes, Inc., Sole Licensee. All Rights Reserved. Used With Permission.

The polygons stated before describe the conducting patterns, except for the second measure, where three eighth notes are grouped together in the first beat. To indicate this beat, a circle, representing a larger number of divisions, reminds me to make that beat longer. It also places the choir's cues each on the first beat. The diagrams look like this:

PART TWO: The Mechanics of Conducting

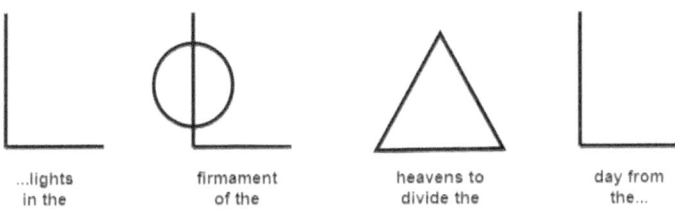

| ...lights in the | firmament of the | heavens to divide the | day from the... |

Again, I mark this with a green highlighter, so that I can see the music underneath the shapes. After

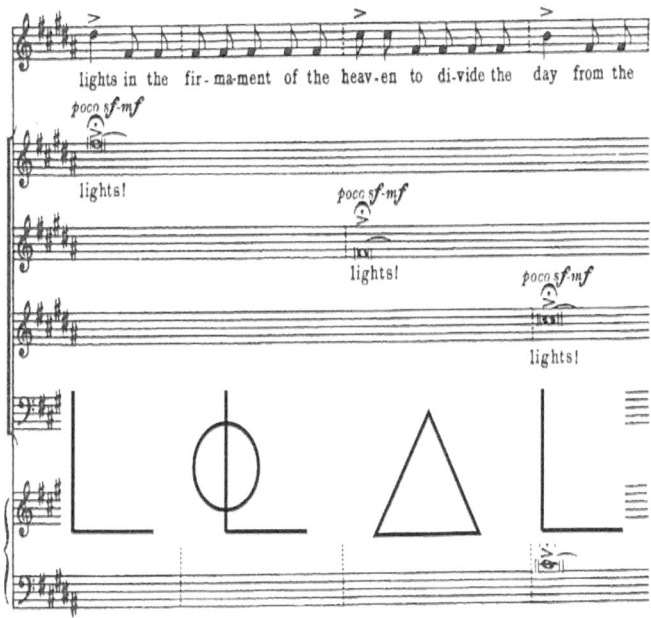

adding these markings, it becomes much easier to conduct this excerpt. Here are what the hands should do:

Conducting Different Meters

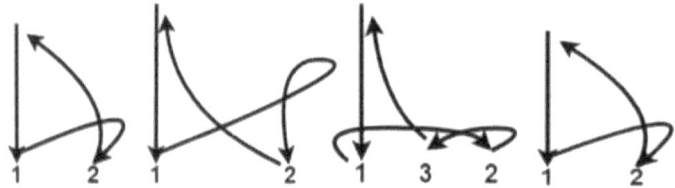

This next example, taken from the handbell piece *Dorian Dance* by Michael Joy, employs multiple patterns in a fast progression. The eighth note beaming tells which patterns to use. In the first measure, the treble clef line shows eighth notes divided in groups of four and is marked 4/4. In the second, third and fourth measures (70-72) the time signature switches to 8/8, and the eighth notes are grouped 3+3+2. First, we mark the eighth notes in groups of twos and threes, as was done in the Copland.

PART TWO: The Mechanics of Conducting

Dorian Dance, by Michael Joy. Irmo, SC: Jeffers Handbell Supply, Inc., 2003. All rights reserved. Used with permission.

Next, we create diagrams. Looking at the first measure, there are four sets of two eighth notes, so we use a FOUR pattern. The next measure, marked 8/8, has the eighth notes divided into three groups of 3+3+2 eighth notes. This means we need to use a THREE pattern. To indicate that beats one and two have three eighth notes each, a circle is used on the diagrams.

Conducting Different Meters

To conduct these patterns, we use a variety of regular and irregular shapes. Here are the diagrams of these patterns:

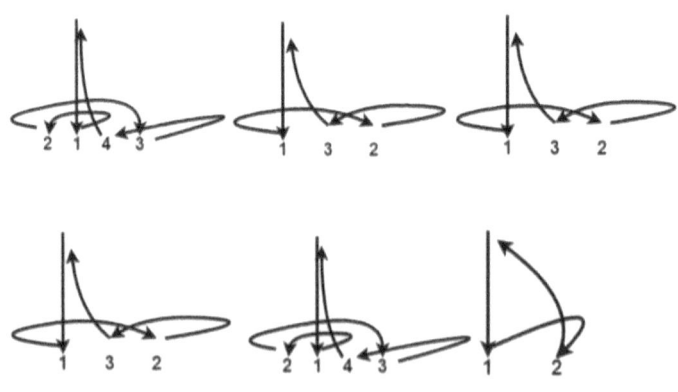

PART TWO: The Mechanics of Conducting

Another great example needing multiple patterns is *Magnificat* by Jonathan Willcocks (b. 1953). It keeps the conductor on his toes because of the changing meters! Here is the score, with the meter markings:

Magnificat by Jonathan Willcocks, © 1997 Lorenz Corporation/Roger Dean Publishing Company (admin. by Music Services). All Rights Reserved. Used by Permission.

Using a highlighter to draw the diagrams helps easily identify the pattern during the rehearsal or performance. In a single glance, I can tell that the first two measures are conducted with a FOUR pattern, followed by a TWO with longer beats, and finally a THREE with a longer third beat.

Conclusion

Using clear patterns, you can lead your group to new and better highs, where they will strive to work for you because they know you are prepared. The shapes quickly remind the correct pattern to show, while freeing the conductor to concentrate on phrases and shaping the melody. As directors we must be ready for the numerous meter changes that await us.

Chapter 6

Preparation

A few months ago, I was invited to a church that was closing its doors. The congregation had served the city for more than fifty years, but like so many places, no longer could sustain its ministry. Instead of referring to the final service as the "last service," it was called "commencement."

Commencement means a culmination ceremony to confer degrees. It means to begin. Beginnings have endings, much like our lives and the lives of others; we end one chapter, and we

Preparation

begin a new one. Out of the church that closed, new life was given to the items in the church such as the organ, the pianos, the music, and all the things within it.

As conductors of volunteer choirs, we spend a tremendous amount of time in preparation for whatever is coming – a service, an anthem, a concert. We spend a lot of time preparing, and we also spend time with preparatory beats. Therefore, we need to know what a preparation is, and when it is used.

The preparatory beat is the beat before a change in the music. Most commonly, it is used to start the choir. The preparatory beat must be in the same speed, motion, articulation, and volume as the notes that are to follow.

When to use a preparatory beat

A preparatory beat is an indication of a change that is about to take place.

Preparations should be used for:
1. The beginning of a score
2. Cues
3. Cutoffs
4. Changes of tempo

General ideas about preparatory beats:

PART TWO: The Mechanics of Conducting

- Preparations should be executed in the manner of the new idea approaching in the music.
- Preparations should take place one beat before the change.
- Preparations should be done either with the left hand or occasionally with both hands.
- Preparations should include some sort of lift toward the top of the beat patterns.
- Preparations should generally follow beat patterns; if the change happens on beat one, the preparation should be a lift that resembles beat four in the left hand. If the change happens on beat four, the preparation should be a lift that resembles beat three in the left hand.

Types of preparations

Invitation in preparation

When working with an ensemble that uses breath – a choir, band, piano accompanist, or other group – use the preparation to mimic breathing. Also, be sure to physically breathe with the ensemble. This creates a sense of empathy between you and the ensemble.

Preparation

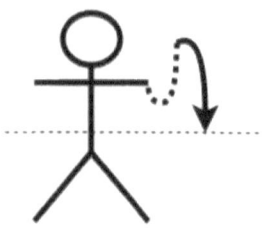

Reference point preparation

When conducting string players, percussion ensembles, and handbell players, use a definitive point that shows exactly where the ictus falls. This gives the players a reference point as to where all other beats occur. Failure to do this will result in a tempo that is slower than you may have intended.

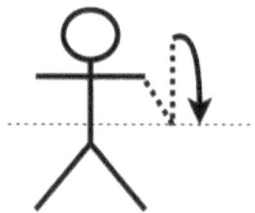

Specific preparatory beats

At the beginning of a score

When starting a piece of music, an excerpt, or anything, that start is preceded by the preparation. Preparations can be done by either one hand or two, and, as has been already stated, must be in the character of the music that is to follow on the first beat.

PART TWO: The Mechanics of Conducting

How many beats?

So many new or untrained conductors that I have worked with use an *entire measure* to prepare. This only works for handbells. For choirs, it is a *total waste of time.* For orchestras, it depends on their familiarity with you. Most of the time, use one beat, as a preparatory beat, in the manner, speed and intent of the upcoming phrase.

Before a cue

A preparatory beat before a cue is the most common use. If the cue is soft, mirror the right hand with the left. If the cue is loud and slow, use both hands, mirrored, and pointed toward the section(s) receiving the cue. If the cue is fast, lift the left hand on the beat before while facing the section about to receive the cue.

When an entrance happens off the beat, use a preparatory beat just like a cue. It stays in the manner of the music being conducted. A word of caution: When creating a preparation for an off-beat, be gentle; becoming overzealous on the preparatory beat will cause the singers to accidentally sing *on* the beat!

Preparation

Changing time from fast to slow

*Fast to slow, starting on
beat four.*

This preparation is easier than the reverse. Using both hands, raise the arms in the speed of the new tempo, and execute the new tempo by using a longer beat.

Changing time signatures slow to fast

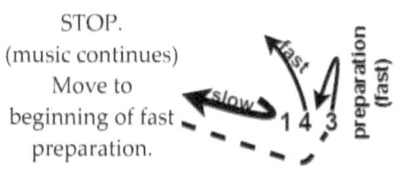

*Slow to fast, starting on
beat four.*

To prepare and execute this kind of change, completely stop beating the pattern at least two beats before the change, then as the new tempo approaches, indicate the preparatory beat in the manner and speed of the new tempo.

PART TWO: The Mechanics of Conducting

Breath in Preparations

The breath is an integral part to preparations – sometimes. In some schools of conducting, one should always breathe when performing a preparatory gesture. The breath should be in the speed and manner of the upcoming phrase. In my experience, strings, winds, and choir all enjoy seeing the empathy of a breath and perform better because of this process. When breathing with the ensemble, remember to breathe low as though preparing to sing the part.

Percussion ensembles, such as handbell choirs, are different. Breathing during a preparatory beat when conducting a handbell choir usually causes the players to rush the beats.

Conclusion

Preparatory beats:
- Are used at the beginning of a score, cues, cutoffs and changes of tempos.
- Should be in the manner and style of the upcoming selection of music.
- Use a breath for non-percussion and no string instruments, breathe. If using percussion or strings, do not breathe during the preparation beat.
- Have are two methods for changing beats. Either use a slower preparatory beat, or stop

Preparation

conducting completely, and use a fast-preparatory beat right before the music changes tempo.

Preparatory beats prepare the choir for what is to come. It is one of the most powerful signals to give to them, along with using the left hand.

Chapter 7

The Left Hand

Now that we have our beat patterns and we know more about motion, we add the left hand. The left hand is used for mirroring, accents, dynamics, and cues, but the most important part of what the conductor does – especially with volunteers – is to cue.

As said before, I'm left-handed. I throw baseballs, write, use a hammer, and pick up coffee cups with my left hand. I look at people writing with their right hand and wonder *how do they do that?* It seems so…unnatural. For the right-handed person, the feeling I'm told, is mutual. So when we have to use the non-dominant hand independently in conducting, it requires a lot of practice. As such, the left hand – or using both hands – will require some practice to get better.

First, we must talk about what to do with the left hand when it is not busy. At one time, I had no idea what one is supposed to do with the left hand when it is resting. This resulted in what I call the resting position.

Resting position

Resting position is where the left hand sits near the ictus when it is not being used.

Left hand in ready position

PART TWO: The Mechanics of Conducting

Cues

There are two main jobs that the conductor has during performance: to start and stop the ensemble and to cue the ensemble. People feel much more secure about entrances, especially entrances after long periods of inactivity, when they see the conductor look at them and bring them in. It is the most powerful instrument in our arsenal of gestures.

Cues must be toward the group and high enough so that they stand out. Here are four examples: one for each beat.

Cue on beat 1   Cue on beat 2

The Left Hand

Cue on beat 3   Cue on beat 4

Use of the eyes

When one is cuing the instrumentalists or singers, one must look at them. It is easy to get distracted at the wonders of music making, or at the music on the printed page – so it is important to train not to do this, to remember this critical component.

Even the most advanced groups sometimes need cues, especially after long periods of silence. Instrumentalists are somewhat less needy in this

PART TWO: The Mechanics of Conducting

regard, *but not always*. Often, string players say to me that they are not used to long gaps of silence like the brass players! Vocalists *especially* need cues, usually more cues than the instrumentalists. Take this opening line from the *Mass for Four Voices* by

William Byrd (c1539/40-1623).

William Byrd. *Mass for Four Voices,* edited by Carlos Rodríguez Otero. Distributed under the terms of the Choral Public Domain Library License (http://www.cpdl.org)

One would expect to cue each section upon entrance, first the altos, then soprano, then tenor. If this were played by a brass quartet, three cues are all that would be required.

The Left Hand

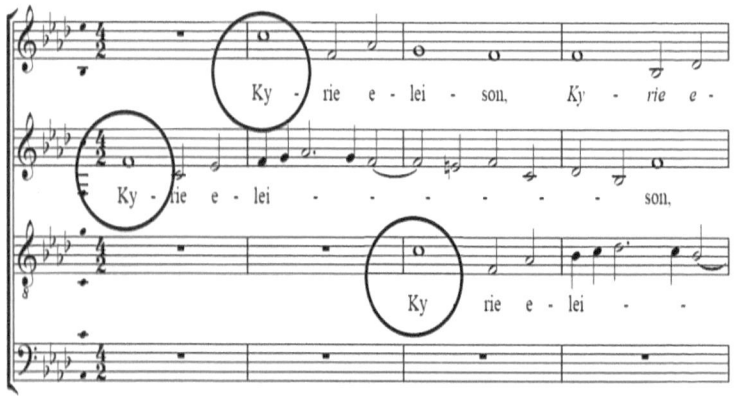

Singers need more attention because of the constant breath support needed to sustain these delicate lines, so at the beginning of new phrases an additional cue is required. Here, the sopranos receive a *second* cue, though they are already singing.

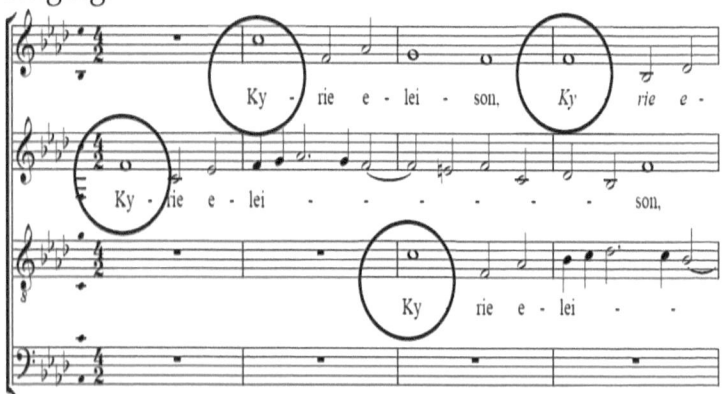

Types of cues

There are three types of cues:

PART TWO: The Mechanics of Conducting

1. The invitation
2. The direct
3. The point

Cues can be accomplished by looking and breathing in the direction of the section. Using the hands, we can reinforce the use of the eyes. Using almost a mirroring motion, lift the left hand and, instead of bringing it downward toward the ictus, bring the hand outward toward the section with the cue, with a slight downward motion. *Most of the time*, breathe in the preparatory beat. As said before, in some cases such as a percussion ensemble or bell choir, do not breathe, as the players could accidentally come in early or late. If you have both percussion and winds/voices/strings, breathe in the beat before. Your players and singers will thank you for it.

1. The invitation

This type of cue is used to invite the group to begin. This involves scooping the left hand toward the section.

2. The direct

The second way, better for more rhythmic entrances, involves tapping toward the group, as though you were going to tap them with the eraser of a pencil. I make an "OK" sign and open my fingers. This works especially well if the cue is not on a strong beat.

1. The point

The third, perhaps most direct and difficult to ignore method, is to point. I have found this works very well with amateur choirs. They rarely miss when I do this and think that I am totally focused on that section. Whichever way you choose, the cue starts the sound. Next, we will discuss how to stop the sound.

Cut-offs

The three types of cutoffs are:
1. Direct - the dramatic type of cutoff.
2. Indirect - a middle of the road cutoff.
3. Phrase release - right before a gesture of syncopation or just showing a breath.

Both types of cut-off gestures mean *stop*. A stop comes at the end of a phrase, at the end of a piece of music, or at the end of a section of music. No one likes to be cut off, whether it is on the freeway, after talking too long, or in music, but the cut-off serves the important point of getting the sound out of the way. Though there are only three types of cut-offs, there are numerous ways to use them.

Cut-offs need to be made in the same manner and shape as the note that it ends. They need to be precise, prepared and pointed, especially as the music becomes more aggressive or rhythmic.

However, cut-offs can be an awful point of the music, as well as a propellant forward at the same time. After a recent performance of Haydn's *Lord Nelson Mass*, I wrote the choir the following morning:

The Left Hand

When in the middle, I get to just turn and look at you - I see when you are right there, with all the right words. I know about the excitement and acceleration that happened and having to hold you back. I know that someone - thank goodness - remembered to sit down at the beginning of Qui Tollis.

But mostly I remember just looking at you, and you looking at me, and we sang together. And for one moment, nothing else mattered. Politics and sugar cookies and the Astros and my mystery novel were all a million miles away last night.

Poof! Suddenly, it was done. I felt like last night I got to take it all in for a little bit. Music is like that, isn't it? Suddenly we are sailors in the Royal Navy trying to defeat Napoleon, until that final moment, where I remember

PART TWO: The Mechanics of Conducting

to conduct the little backwards cut-off so it'll last just a second longer.
You were well-praised, from what I heard, by the audience, last night. You should be proud of the work you did, and the people you touched.

All good things come to an end – including every performance.

1. Direct cutoff

The direct cutoff sharply ends the sounds in a final punctuation. It starts by a preparation followed by a strong downward motion in the left hand. Use a preparation on the beat before, followed by a chop downward on the ending beat.

  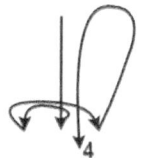

2. Indirect cutoff

For a more nuanced cutoff where the sound may be gentler, an indirect cutoff may be ideal. For these types of cutoffs, bring one or both hands up and in toward the body. Bring the hands down to the ictus, outlining a letter "C" with the hand (forwards in the right hand, backwards in the left).

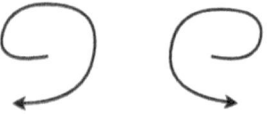

3. *Phrase release*

The phrase release can be done on a note to remind the ensemble to breathe or lift. This is accomplished by touching the ictus and immediately lifting the hand up and away from the ictus. Following the phrase release, begin moving toward the next beat. Phrase releases may slow the tempo, but movement away from the release toward the next beat should be done in the same manner and tempo as before the release.

Cutoffs are not as important as cues, but nevertheless they are an important act of conducting. After all, our main jobs are to start the sound, remind the choir to sing, and – from time to time – tell the choir to stop.

The gesture of syncopation

The gesture of syncopation creates both a stop and a jumping off point. Gestures of syncopation have their own nuances and issues, and though they are like phrase cut-offs, they have a forward momentum attached to them. The main

PART TWO: The Mechanics of Conducting

point is to show an entrance or notes that happen *after* a beat. In this way, it shows the *rest* that precedes an entrance. It acts as a placeholder.

Bach, *Cantata No. 140*, opening movement. New York: G. Schirmer, (ca. 1925). Accessed via IMSLP. Public Domain.

In this example, a gesture of syncopation is appropriate in all three measures – first for the tenors, then the altos, and finally the basses, while the soprano continues singing the main hymn tune. One can always use the hands to accentuate the rest. The steps to create this are below:

The Left Hand

1. Before the gesture of syncopation, have the hand in a downward, closed position.

2. Now touching the ictus, open the hand.

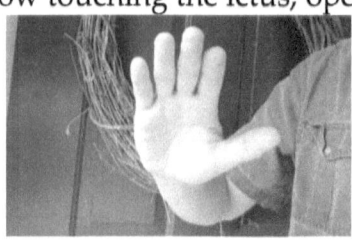

Combining gestures of syncopation and other motions

In this example from Johannes Brahms's (1833-1897) *How Lovely Are Thy Dwellings*, the gesture of syncopation happens in the bass line, after cuing the soprano on the third beat.

PART TWO: The Mechanics of Conducting

Brahms, "How Lovely Are Thy Dwellings." New York: G. Schirmer, 1907. Public Domain.

In this case, the emphasis is on beat 1. Approach it with a preparatory gesture on beat three of the previous measure. For sake of the example, ignore the soprano line at first to concentrate on the cue in the bass line. Use the open-hand gesture on beat 1 of the second measure.

This example is more complicated – and more common - because immediately preceding the gesture of syncopation in the second measure, there is a cue in the soprano. Sometimes, music, when it gets more exciting, has multiple cues that happen on top of one another. In this case, a cue on beat 3 and a gesture of syncopation on beat one. This means that a preparatory beat must happen on

The Left Hand

beat two for the soprano cue, and a preparatory happens on beat 3 for the bass cue. Below is a breakdown of the gestures needed.

1. Measure 1, Beat 2: left hand comes up to prepare for cue.
2. Measure 1, Beat 3: Left hand points to sopranos as cue on beat three; right hand comes up to prepare gesture of syncopation on beat 1 of the next measure.
3. Measure 2, Beat 1: the gesture of syncopation occurs with right hand emphasizing the beginning of the beat.

The gesture of syncopation is an emphasis on the beginning of the beat so that the choir will come in after the beat begins. Sometimes, these come in conjunction with additional cues in other

PART TWO: The Mechanics of Conducting

parts, so it is important to be able to do these and cues in both hands. Choristers rely very heavily on your ability to execute them.

Conclusion

Cues play an incredibly important part for volunteer choirs. So much so, that one of my choristers made me laugh when, after stopping during rehearsal, said with the best southern drawl she could muster, "Honey can you just go ahead and cue me there, 'cause I haven't got a clue when to start singing…"

Therefore, we cue.

Chapter 8

The Baton

My first baton, a mix of cork, graphite, and a heavy tip that dipped unceremoniously to the floor, granted me ideas and dreams of conducting great concerts.

It was perfect.

Taking conducting for the first time, I learned the patterns and studied cues and using both hands. It was the course I had most wanted to take when I started college. I had seen the orchestral conductor wave his baton and watched the eloquence in which he elicited great melodies out of the student orchestra. I do not think the man ever knew my name.

I conducted along with the great recordings on the classical music station while in the car. Beethoven? Dvorak? Haydn? I was a master in my own mind! But I had no idea how to lead. I just wanted eloquent gesture. It would take longer to turn that eloquent gesture into great leading.

The meaning of the baton

The conductor's seeming dictatorship on the ensemble is absolute; nothing symbolizes this as does the baton. The baton is a symbol, yes, but it also is a tool. In this case, it is an extension of the arm and, therefore, an extension of the *self*.

This is both a good and bad thing – we will, in discussing the warm-up talk about the deflation of the *self* through breath and through the release of the ego. The baton is no different; in the wrong hands it is a symbol of the tyranny that orchestral players experienced at the beginning of the twentieth century under Toscanini, Klemperer, or others. In the right hands, it is a tool. In fact, it is a magnifier; it is an extension of the arm used for far-away musicians to see the gestures you make.

Why does one need to use a baton? Two reasons:

First, larger ensembles – such as those with orchestras or when the group is far away from the conductor – need a much larger, more visible reference point. Using the baton in these circumstances acts as a magnifier, increasing the range of visibility.

Second, precise beats – such as those with percussion ensembles or handbells – make the baton especially useful. A particularly wonderful style of conducting called "focal point conducting," proposed by John Paynter where each of the beats falls in the same place, is wonderfully suited to the baton. See the example below, divided into two parts to see the point easier.

Choosing the baton

Aside from references to young wizards of the *Harry Potter* series, there is nothing magical about the baton choice, except to get one. My first baton was made of cork and fiberglass; it travelled well in a notebook spiral. Like an ugly, rusted car travelling from point A to point B, any baton will

PART TWO: The Mechanics of Conducting

do to get started, but eventually you will want one best suited to a preferred grip, balance, and length.

The baton serves two purposes: first, to magnify the motion of the hand and wrist (thereby saving energy), and second, to decrease the amount of extra motion needed to show and remind the ensemble of what needs to be done (again, saving energy).

1. Grip

Batons come in many shapes and sizes. Try several different ones before you choose your ideal shape.

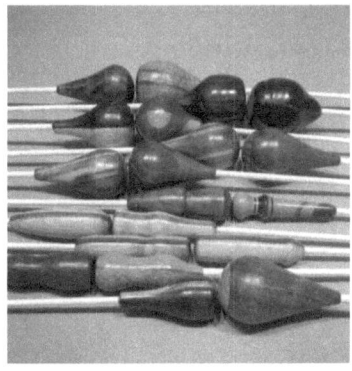

The Baton

A set of conducting baton handles from Etsy.

One of my favorite types is the teardrop shaped baton, which is widely available. (I have multiple batons both for size and convenience; I even have one that my partner gave me with multiple wood colors that I use specifically for his handbell choir.) Teardrop shaped grips balance extremely well and can point outward without too much effort.

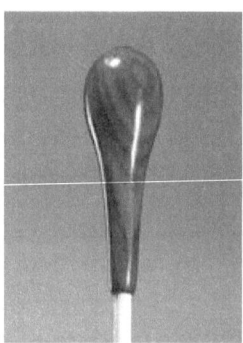

Teardrop grip

My go-to, absolute favorite baton grip is the round grip, shown below.

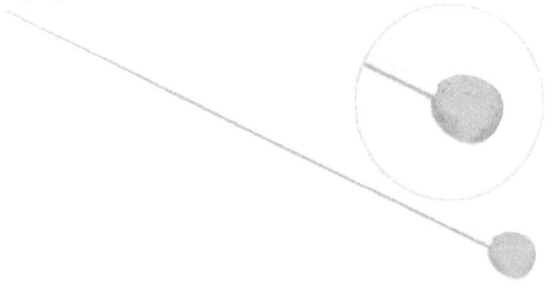

Round grip

PART TWO: The Mechanics of Conducting

With the round grip, the fingers can manipulate the stick easily, saving motion and extra energy. On my own baton with the ball grip, the balance is sacrificed – a worthy price for ease of manipulation, which brings us to the next criteria.

2. Balance

The best batons have a balance point (or fulcrum) at the end of the grip. If the baton's fulcrum is further down the shaft, it will constantly want to dip downward. Personally, I prefer grip shape over balance point, but an ideal baton has both.

3. Length

This is most dependent on what kind of ensemble you are intending to conduct. Is your group smaller, such as a chamber orchestra or small band or bell choir? Use a smaller shaft, such as 360mm (13-14 inches). The large choir/orchestra combinations, or when your group is far away (such as a marching band or an unusual performance setup like instrumentalists in a balcony) need at least 400mm (15 or more inches). *This is the most important criteria for choosing which baton to use.*

The Baton

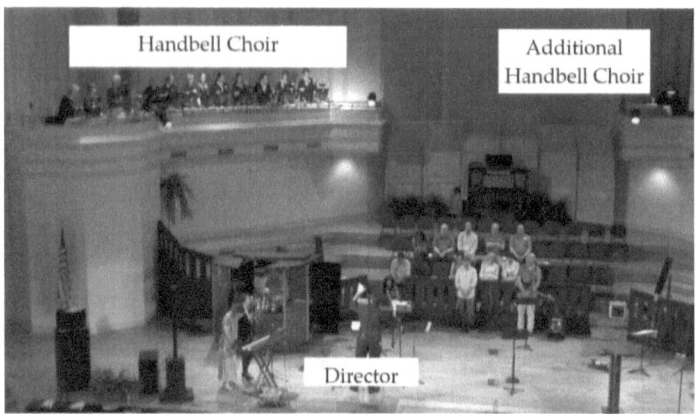

This setup needed a large baton, because the conductor is on a different floor from the handbell choir.

Holding the baton

Look at the grip pictures. In the first, the conductor is holding the baton with the two fingers and thumb. The baton can be manipulated with the thumb and the first finger. If conducting an orchestra, the baton should point directly out, so that those sitting immediately to the conductor's left and right have a clear view of the gesture.

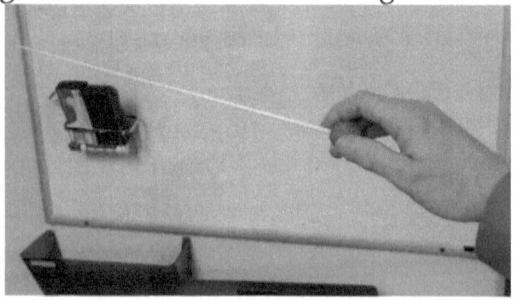

PART TWO: The Mechanics of Conducting

In this photo, the grip is relaxed, but the hand is positioned to the side so that the baton stands straight out.

In this next photo, the conductor's hand has palm facing downward. Though the last two fingers are pointed up, the conductor has more control over the stick because the hand is palm down and the fingers can manipulate the stick.

In this example the grip is tight, and as a result, the baton is turned sideways, making it difficult for the first violins, seated at the conductor's left, and celli, seated at the conductor's left, to see the baton.

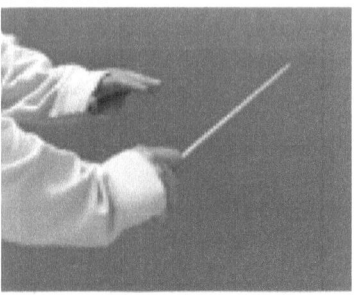

Conclusion

The baton is a tool that is used to amplify the hand and arm movement. With a larger ensemble, it is more important to have a larger baton that can be seen. Not only does this increase the conductor's reach, but it also allows the conductor to use less energy by manipulating the baton with only the fingers. This way, you can conduct those long Wagner operas, big oratorios, and those ensembles far away in the balcony!

Remember when holding a baton, it is *an extension of you*, and should be used as such.

Chapter 9

Stops and Starts

Maybe you felt a call early in your life that said you should direct a volunteer choir. Maybe it came in college or after.

In April of 2013, I made a phone call – namely because I had just taken a job as a college professor in a small town; the same town and same job I had been in many years earlier. On a day in late April my boss, whom I admired, and who had just hired me for the second time, told me that my old church was waiting to give me my job back.

Stops and Starts

Was I sure about doing this SECOND *job* AGAIN!*???* I had been overwhelmed with work when I was there before. My mind said, "One man, one job...," but here I was, calling my old church, which I had left ten years ago when I moved. A wonderful woman answered the phone, and after I told her my name and that I had been at this same church years ago, she gasped and said I was the answer to prayer.

I didn't feel like the answer to prayer.

Before long, I was back at my former church, working with my same choir members and combining them with other churches to produce larger works. I was taking organ lessons and preaching sermons. I stayed above the day-to-day fray of the church and enjoyed my job. I conducted, sang, advised, prayed with others, and belonged. For the first time in my career, I felt *needed* and *respected* as a person and as an employee.

Within six months there was a constant stream of chaos in my academic life. My boss had retired, and my college job was full of strife. Despite this, I lacked the courage to step away from the university. After all, I had trained and worked hard to get there. As the chaos of my academic job got worse, I would go to the church, spend time working on the library, talking to my senior pastor or the associate pastor, practicing the organ, and preparing for the next musical undertaking with the church choir or combined-church group. Two years later, my career needed to change because I had changed. As the college year ended, I was convinced that better things were ahead outside the classroom. The fear was gone, and in its place was a new freedom that God 'was clearly in control. I never looked back.

As I interviewed for a new, full-time church music position, I realized how much more relaxed I could be as a spiritual person who loved music, rather than as a commodity who held a doctorate and would boost college rankings and assessment. Though I did not know where my next paycheck would come from, my friends circled around, kept me busy, and encouraged me.

The position I accepted opened as a total surprise. During those few months of not working, I had had time to re-examine my career, my life, and my work. It was a rather dramatic pause, not unlike some in music. Pauses in our life, and in our careers, can be wonderful things, because they can anticipate new, exciting plans. Never be afraid of the pauses.

The fermata

The fermata – a pause – remains a complex problem for conductors because there are so many ways to handle them. Fermatas are simple in their concept: *STOP*. But how is this accomplished? What do fermatas all have in common?

Characteristics common to fermatas

Fermatas must be approached.

In some situations, there is a gradual slowdown, while others are sudden holds, but all fermatas are entered in some fashion.

Fermatas must be held.

The hold is of different lengths and times, and can depend on the conductor, the hall, or other situation.

Fermatas require prior planning to execute.

Like all conducting, you must decide as to how to conduct the fermata before encountering it during the rehearsal or performance.

Types of fermatas

There are many types of fermatas, but we will focus on the two most common.
1. Cutoff fermata
2. Re-beat fermata

Sadly, they all look alike! Each of these fermatas require different motions and different preparations. All of them need to be identified before attempting to conduct.

PART TWO: The Mechanics of Conducting

4. *The Cutoff fermata*

This fermata happens where the ensemble needs to stop sound before moving to the next beat. The fermata, in this case, must last longer than one beat.

Johann Sebastian Bach, *Wie bin ich doch so herzlich froh,* from *Cantata No. 1.* Leipzig: Breitkopf and Härtel, 1851. Accessed via IMSLP. Public Domain.

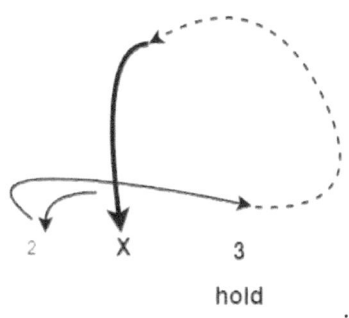

Stops and Starts

5. *The Re-beat fermata*

Much like the cutoff fermata, the Re-beat fermata takes place where the ensemble needs to stop sound before moving to the next beat. However, the fermata only lasts for one beat, and moves on, after a cut-off.

Bach, final chorale from *St. John Passion*. Leipzig: Breitkoph and Härtel, 1882. Accessed via IMSLP. Public Domain.

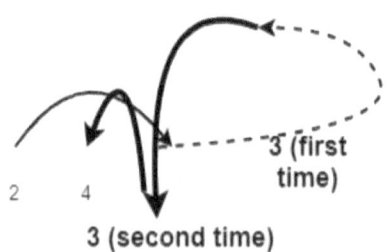

This example, taken from the final chorale of the *St. John Passion* by Bach, lasts for one beat, and immediately moves on. When conducting this

PART TWO: The Mechanics of Conducting

type, approach the fermata in the pattern, raise both hands to hold the fermata on beat three, then conduct the same beat again as a cut-off, moving forward into beat four and to the next measure.

Most important to starting and stopping the fermata is planning what kind of fermata it is and how to conduct it. With some practice, each of these will get easier.

Recitative

Recitatives – following singers in a non-metered phrase – are some of the most advanced areas of conducting. Recitative is sung dialogue that uses sparse accompaniment. For volunteers, works such as *Messiah* by George Frederic Handel (1685-1759), and *Amahl and the Night Visitors* by Gian Carlo Menotti (1911-2007) use recitatives. Here is an example:

Handel, "There were shepherds abiding in the field," from *Messiah.* New York: G. Schirmer, 1912. Accessed via IMSLP. Public Domain.

From time to time, we will face these sections where our gestures must be accurate and are dependent upon the speed of a soloist. Each situation is different, but it's important to look at some similarities and some gestures that will become important in your ever-increasing arsenal of gesture.

Common recitative solutions

In a recitative, your job is to keep the ensemble together and moving forward. This means there are some new gestures to learn to help keep the ensemble informed.

The dead gesture

In orchestras and bands, it is imperative that the first beat be displayed, so every player, whether performing or at rest, knows exactly what beat is occurring. The dead gesture is a small first beat, meant only to mark time. If the first beat is not played by anyone, a dead gesture is used. See the *Messiah* example, now altered to include where dead gestures ("dead") and cues (arrows) go.

PART TWO: The Mechanics of Conducting

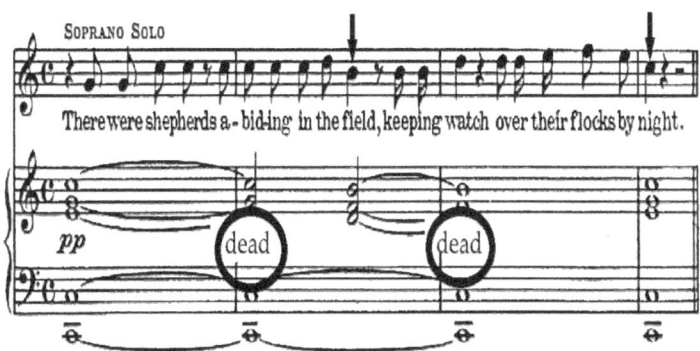

The dead gesture can be employed at the beginning of measures two and three to mark the downbeat. Where there are arrows, provide a cue for the instrumentalists. In the second measure, a preparation occurs (following the soloist) on beat 2, cuing beat three (again, following the soloist), and a dead beat on the next beat 1. The pattern would look something like this:

Stops and Starts

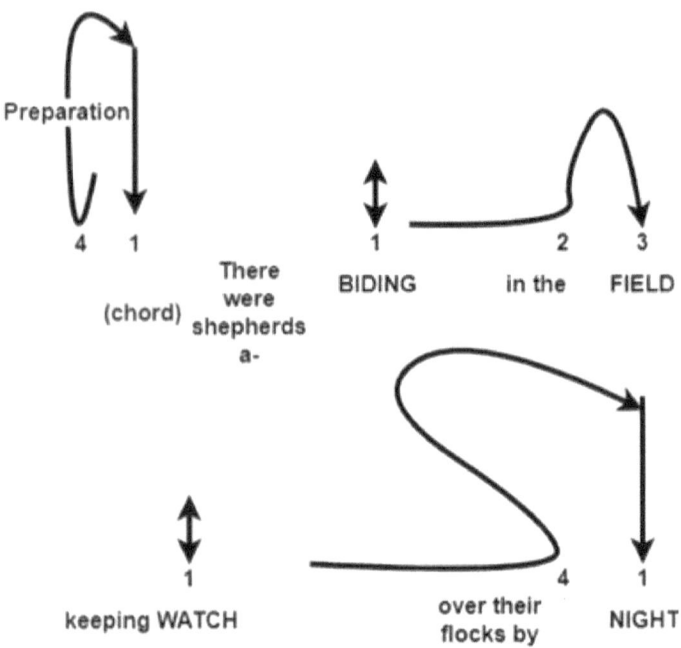

Sometimes, especially in baroque music, the cadences – the ends of phrases – are handled differently than how they look on the page. For instance, the end of "Comfort Ye," the opening recitative from *Messiah* looks like this on the page:

PART TWO: The Mechanics of Conducting

Handel, "Comfort Ye," from *Messiah*.

but it is supposed to sound like this:

(Author's editing.)

Stops and Starts

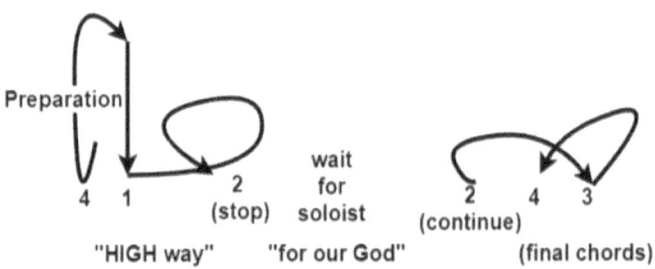

The tenor finishes singing before the final two chords are played. In today's performance practice, more conductors choose to perform the second version. To conduct this the hand completely stops moving (the dead gesture) in the second full measure. After each of the two final chords, the conductor cuts off the note using an indirect cutoff.

Conclusion

Though we all may not perform large scale works for chorus every year, most of us will face a Christmas *Messiah* performance at least once in our careers. For this and more, we should be ready.

PART THREE:

Preparing for Rehearsal

Chapter 10

Before the First Rehearsal

You have your choir. You have the accompanist, the music, folders, chairs, and a place for rehearsal. Now what? These are other background items that need to be addressed to create a good volunteer choir rehearsal: the space, the order, the connections, and the musical ideas.

PART THREE: Preparing for rehearsal.

Space

Different people have ideas how to structure their rehearsal space. In one place, I came in and the ladies were on risers, and the men sat on the floor. Some choirs sing in quartets; others place the men in the back row, and the sopranos and altos on the front rows.

What works:

For volunteers, two things are paramount: to hear one another, especially if there is a strong singer, and to not have to sing alone. The latter, for volunteer singers, is essential. I have mostly subscribed, in a volunteer choir, to having tenors and basses on the back row because lower frequencies travel further than higher frequencies (and there are in many choirs more ladies than men). I also believe in splitting sections, especially in larger choirs. This helps me, as conductor, to point cues because they're always in the same place.

Sometimes, space is minimal. After Hurricane Harvey destroyed our church in 2017, we rehearsed in a small chapel. I arranged it having measured the chairs and walls, to create a diagram, using sticky notes for the chairs, and drawings for the walls, like this:

Before the First Rehearsal

One inch represents one foot in the space, and after a little work, more than fifty people can be fitted into this small chapel – a live room with a cement floor making the choir sound like five hundred. The result looked like this:

For concerts, seat the singers in a seating chart, placing singers in a different place than in rehearsal. There are a few rules here: put the singers who may have to exit the choir during the performance on the ends. This includes soloists, bell choir members, additional children's choir

PART THREE: Preparing for rehearsal.

directors or ensemble members that must get up during the performance (like a narrator). The strongest singers go in the middle of the row, so that other singers can hear them. Finally, try to put weaker singers next to stronger ones and new members next to experienced ones.

What does not work:
- Putting newcomers together.
- Singing in quartets where a singer is not sitting next to someone else from his or her part. (This applies to volunteers only; for seasoned singers, singing in quartets can be very satisfying.)
- Putting the men in front of the ladies.
- Allowing the singers to seat themselves when performance time nears.

Order

Volunteer choirs, especially religious choirs, are in a constant battle of passing out music, handing in music, retrieving music from volunteers, contacting people to have them return their music, and the constant flow of paper and music that comes in and out. A few questions need to be answered first:
- Does the choir have folders? Are those folders kept in your rehearsal space or with the members?

- What are the current procedures for passing out and returning music?
- How does the choir receive music? Does the choir purchase their own music? Does that music get purchased from you or from a local (or internet) dealer? Do you have purchase information for those that might want to buy their own music anyway?
- Does your accompanist have a way to return music to you?
- Do you have someone to help in getting the music back from people who may not have it?
- Do you have a list of emails and phone numbers to retrieve music?

A few suggestions:

I have had choirs buy music, keep music with them, use folder slots, and had copies lying on a table for them to pick up at the beginning of rehearsal. My best success has been to give the singers a numbered copy in a folder that they leave in the rehearsal space. They are much less likely to lose the music, they can be contacted if it is not returned after use, and they feel a sense of ownership when we go back to the same piece and "their" markings are on "their own" music. Each person in my choir has an assigned number and their music has corresponding numbers. This is a

PART THREE: Preparing for rehearsal.

lot more work, but I do not have to purchase numerous extra copies repeatedly because someone took five copies and left each of them in his folder slot each week (yes, that is a true story), or had to search around because someone wanted an "Alto Copy" of the mass or anthem we are about to rehearse.

My predecessor at my current position started the method of numbering folders and music, and after a short adjustment, I realized this was an excellent method of constant music filing and organization. Each person has anthems with their folder number "pre-stuffed" before rehearsal. As the Sunday anthem approaches, the singers are asked to pass the anthem in after our final rehearsal that Wednesday night. On Sunday morning, the anthems are placed by the robes in numerical order, so we can rehearse right in the sanctuary. After the service, the anthems are collected, along with any leftovers on the table by the robes, and no one accidentally takes their used anthem home with them. It is a little more work, but with a volunteer or two, the reward is always winding up with the same number of anthems after each service.

Connections

When Hurricane Harvey slammed into Southeast Texas dropping over 50 inches of rain on

Before the First Rehearsal

us, it was imperative to be able to quickly contact the choir: first to tell them there was no rehearsal, and then to give them updates and ask them to help volunteer to dry out music, take home robes for cleaning, and other essential projects to bring the church back on line. I eventually subscribed to an email site and use that to regularly contact my choir and send out the rehearsal order. Today I have an "everyone" group, Monday night bells, Wednesday night bells, Chancel Choir, and Community Chorus lists. When COVID-19 struck, with one email I was able to cancel rehearsals and contact everyone in all the choirs, preparing newsletters and short videos to help lift spirits.

On Monday of every week, I send out a rehearsal order for the Chancel Choir and Community Chorus. I have a short blurb about something coming up, a few words from me or ideas (sometimes musical, sometimes not), and – most importantly – the order of pieces for this week. This gives the choir some knowledge as to what is coming up, giving a sense of purpose, and makes me start thinking about our upcoming rehearsal. What do I want to accomplish? How will I make that happen? Is there a piece coming up that needs more time? Have I picked enough music for the foreseeable future?

PART THREE: Preparing for rehearsal.

As I write this, the world is clasped in a pandemic; I have not seen my choir in weeks. Now, more than ever, just as with hurricanes, floods, ice storms, earthquakes, or other natural disasters, it is imperative that I keep connected with the choir, and them to one another. This is the longest disaster-hiatus we have ever had, so I sent an email called "how are you doing?" along with a video of my flower garden, plants, dogs and things I do to pass the time. I invited the choir members to send me some words, pictures or their own videos telling about how they are passing the time. Though this is not our first disaster as a choir, in a collective disaster experience like this that we are going through, connection is more important now as ever. We meet online each week now, just to stay connected.

A few tips on connectivity:

- Have an email list and send a rehearsal order weekly.
- Have a birthday list and celebrate birthdays once a month at the end of rehearsal.
- Keep stationary and write notes and cards – as the director. Your contact with the choir boosts camaraderie.
- Send text messages and make phone calls to choir members who may be having health

problems or difficulties in getting to rehearsal.
- At the end of rehearsal, have some sort of closing where everyone participates – a prayer, a closing song, joys and concerns, a short gratitude statement, or a unison benediction all work to build this common sense of community.

Musical ideas (how to prepare for rehearsal)

For our purposes we assume familiarity with the score already. In the hour or two before rehearsal, review at the piano what the music should sound like. Play through the parts, noting difficult selections, reviewing hard skips and fast-moving runs. Also look at ways to identify starting pitches of a new selection, relying on other sections' notes to guide the singer to his or her first note of a new selection.

Sticky notes and a written rehearsal plan are your best friends. I call this "me of the past talking to me of the present." The sticky notes show me what page to go to, where the problem is, any notes about possible problems, and what page to go to next. During rehearsal, I tend to forget things easily – problems from last week, new issues, diction, and even note insecurity can get

PART THREE: Preparing for rehearsal.

swept under by more successful selections that come closer to the end of a sung excerpt. When I put sticky notes on the page with comments before rehearsal starts, I know precisely where to go to, and I do not *waste time* searching for the next problem!

- In major works, label the start and end of each selection to work on with a sticky note sticking out from the edge of the book with numbers indicating which area to go to first, second, third, etc.
- Point out difficult selections or passages first, using notes to signal the beginning and ending of the passage, and any techniques that I think should be used such as "Alto and tenor sing together first," or "Bass intonation." These tell where I need to focus first.
- As we get closer to performance time, have the choir sing through the entire movement, song, or selection. While they are singing, place sticky notes in places where the choir needs to review. If it is a long work, compile a list for the next rehearsal, so that the choir knows exactly where the mistakes are and can look at them before rehearsal.

Before the First Rehearsal

- Sticky notes can be taken away when troubled selections improve; often they can be re-used in other places.
- Sticky notes to myself are also helpful for performances to remind which piece comes next, who should be acknowledged at the end of works, or to leave the podium. (Since my memory can be faulty, this helps me to stay on task through the performance.)

A written rehearsal plan is one of the most powerful tools we have at our disposal to make rehearsal move quickly. Days before rehearsal, I write out and send exactly what we will be working on. Here is a recent example:

Choir Retreat - October 12

10:00 - Warm-up
10:05 - Bach Cantata #140 - closing mvt. pg. 59-61 with words
10:15 - **2 part Sectionals** - Bach Cantata #140 - altos and tenors together/sopranos and basses together on opening movement
10:25 - **4 part Sectionals** - Star Carol - all
10:35 - **4 part Sectionals** - Dormi Jesu - all
10:45 - **4 part Sectionals** - God Rest Ye Merry Gentlemen - Harris
10:55 - **Full Rehearsal** - Dormi Jesu - Rutter - final 2 pages

PART THREE: Preparing for rehearsal.

> 11:00 - Bach Cantata #140 - opening movement
> 11:10 - Star Carol
> 11:20 - Personent Hodie – Hoggard
> 11:30 – BREAK

(Bold instructions indicate where the choir members change rooms.)

This tells me and the choir exactly what we will rehearse. Before starting this method, I had a great deal of trouble remembering what we needed to rehearse, and as a result I wasted a lot of rehearsal time.

You may have noticed that I put times on the rehearsal schedule. I do this also so that I do not "drag" rehearsal by continually going over and over a section that remains unfixed. If it gets fixed during the time allotted, great. If not, I can schedule more time for next rehearsal. At this point, I can usually tell how much time it will take on a section of music. This is crucial for rehearsal pacing – I cannot spend too much time on any one part, or the choir gets bored. If the choir gets bored, they will not come back!

Conclusion

The excitement I feel each week over preparing for rehearsal comes from a well-thought plan. I am always eager to see the choir – my gang – and make music with them. Though it requires behind the scenes work – preparing the music, communicating with the choir, readying the space, and setting up the flow of music – they all contribute to making a successful and enjoyable rehearsal. After all, week after week, aren't they coming back to serve their choir, their church, or their community, and enjoying it in the process?

Chapter 11

Approaching a New Score

Score study is a major part of what we do as conductors. If we do not know the music, how are we to teach it?

Earlier, we talked about the five-step process in selecting music for rehearsal, but the first step, becoming acquainted with the music, deserves a little more attention. Here are a few general guidelines I follow:

Approaching a New Score

Guidelines to learn the score

1. Identify the key signature, time signature, mode, and any primary melodies. Break the piece (if long) into sections.
2. Identify any meter changes or tempo changes. Mark them in green.
3. Identify dynamic changes (loud/soft). Mark them in pink (f) or blue (p). If the dynamic stays the same, there is no need to mark it.
4. Identify the melody/melodies. If the music passes the melody around, called *polyphonic music*, mark these entrances in yellow. If the music is polyphonic, create the "conductor's line." This is a melodic line that follows the entrance of every part. Singing through this line traces the "bones" of the work and shows the placement of each cue.
5. Once the conductor's line is set, practice it, along with each of the cues. Then focus on the secondary melodies – the accompaniments. These tend to be harder because they are not as obvious or tuneful and may be more challenging. Play or sing through them and see how they relate to one another.
6. Next, play through any additional countermelodies.

PART THREE: Preparing for Rehearsal.

7. Finally, conduct and cue all parts, being able to switch at will. The motto is, "If I can sing a line *a cappella*, I know it."

Remember, conducting is an *act of acceptance.*

Often, I confront a new score with some trepidation. The notes are new and unfamiliar, and I secretly decide in my mind that I will *never* know it like I knew the last score. This is a terrible mindset that comes to me when I start any new piece.

Total honesty time: If I do not know the score, there is a part of my mind that goes to a negative place, filled with fear and dread. It says I will never know this score as well as *last time.* This phantom seems real and is scary. It reminds me why I will fail and shows every way in which I will fail.

My mind is a little over-dramatic.

It does not seem so in the moment, though. I have worked with other directors who felt the exact same way. No amount of preparation protects me from this fear. Like all fears, it can be conquered by continuing to walk through it. Experience shows me that each new piece has its own challenges and rewards, and within minutes of beginning a new score study I am reminded of my love for the new piece. This time of fear gets

Approaching a New Score

shorter and shorter as I become more and more comfortable with a new score. Learning music isn't easy, and neither is being a conductor, but my worst enemy is not the difficult piece of music out there, or the horrible, critical people that glare in the audience, it's the negative voice in my own head that goes away the second that I start working.

Let's look at the process of learning and editing the opening movement to Bach's *Cantata No. 140*, using the piano-vocal version. Here is the process, broken down, even more extensively than the five-steps discussed earlier.

> 1. ***Identify the key signature, time signature, mode, and any primary melodies.***
> - Key Signature – E flat major
> - Time Signature - 3/4
> - Mode: major.
> - Primary melody: "Sleepers Wake," by Phillipp Nicolai.
>
> 2. ***Identify any meter changes or tempo changes.***
> - The only meter change is the opening tempo indication. (Allegro moderato is an editorial mark, and may be ignored.)
>
> 3. ***Identify dynamic changes (loud/soft).***

PART THREE: Preparing for Rehearsal.

- Dynamics are forte at the beginning, change at A, and change again a few measures afterward.

4. *Identify the melody/melodies.*

- The main melody is in the soprano, but there are numerous cues in the other parts.
- These will need to be addressed when creating the conductor's line.

Approaching a New Score

No. 1. Chorus
[Allegro moderato ♩=80]

PART THREE: *Preparing for Rehearsal.*

Approaching a New Score

Bach, *Cantata No. 140,* opening. Breitkopf und Hartel, 1931. Accessed via IMSLP. Public domain.

5. *Create a "conductor's line."*
- Must include cues including strings, winds and individual entrances.

The conductor's line creates a part that I can sing through and prepares me to conduct each entrance in the opening lines of this work. When I change parts, I cue. Until a new part enters, I

PART THREE: Preparing for Rehearsal.

remain with the part most recently cued. Finally, I cue as I change parts.

Author's rendition of the conductor's line of *Cantata 140*, first movement excerpt.

Approaching a New Score

In our example, the main melody is in the soprano – it is the hymn tune *Wachet Auf, Ruft Uns Die Stimme*. (Sometimes in English it is called "Wake, Awake, for Night is Flying," or "Sleepers Wake for Night Surrounds Us.") Under the melody are several entrances that can be marked for each of the parts.

> **6. Once the conductor's line is set, focus on the secondary melodies, the accompaniments.**

These tend to be harder because they are not the main melody. Play through them or sing through them and see how they relate to one another. Afterward, play through any additional countermelodies.

> **7. Finally, conduct and cue all parts, being able to switch parts at will.**

Again, the motto is "If I can sing a line *a cappella*, I know it." If you do not feel comfortable moving back and forth between lines, go back to the piano and continue practicing until switching parts is automatic.

Sometimes, the conductor's line can be remarkably busy.

In renaissance music or highly contrapuntal pieces, such as in *If Ye Love Me*, by Thomas Tallis

PART THREE: Preparing for Rehearsal.

(1505-1585), the conductor's line remains extremely busy throughout the piece.

Approaching a New Score

PART THREE: Preparing for Rehearsal.

Approaching a New Score

Thomas Tallis, *If Ye Love Me*, London: Novello, 1862.
Accessed via IMSLP. Public domain.

In this case, other than the opening four measures, the conductor's line has many cues, shown below.

PART THREE: Preparing for Rehearsal.

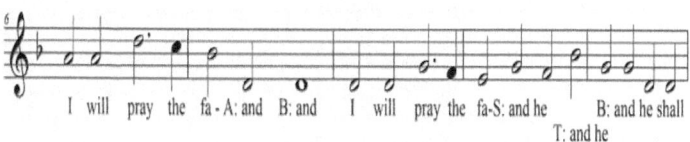

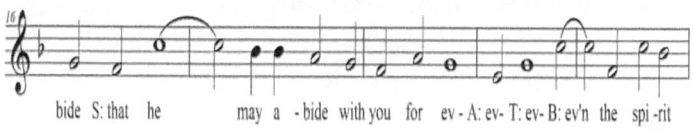
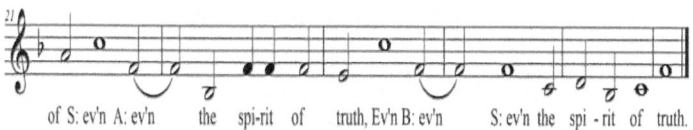

Author's rendition of the conductor's line for *If Ye Love Me.*

Conclusion

Really, there is no "right" way or "wrong" way to study a score, except to *not* study it. The

Approaching a New Score

members of the ensemble, who take time out of their busy weeks to learn the scores, deserve our best. With quick, efficient, and thorough preparation, we will not find ourselves standing in front of them in rehearsal reading the music for the first time. Following the steps outlined will allow us to have some familiarity with a piece of music before the first chorister sets foot in our rehearsal room.

When I first learned to conduct, I often wondered "HOW do we prepare the score?" I was told to sit at the piano and play through each part. Not being the greatest pianist, I spent more time concentrating on the actual playing of open scores than hearing and understanding what needed my gestures. Today, I spend time singing through each part, as I play all the parts. Because I know the parts, I can empathize with my singers. Because I empathize with my singers, I possess the readiness, at a moment's notice, to sing their parts with them or for them.

Chapter 12

Developing the Rehearsal Plan

Nothing can kill a choir faster than a series of bad rehearsals. Bad performances happen, but bad rehearsals – repeated bad rehearsals – can destroy the ensemble. One of the best things I ever learned was how to organize and run a rehearsal. The techniques I use come from years of experience, suggestions from some wonderful conductors and teachers, and regular evaluation and thought about my own rehearsals.

Tips to begin

1. Choose the music.

This seems like an obvious tip, but using the techniques outlined in Chapter 3, choose the music and go through what you are going to rehearse. Do this before every rehearsal so there is no doubt in your mind what the piece sounds like and what needs rehearsing.

2. Time each piece of music.

Of course, picking music means not to choose music that is too long or too short. A typical anthem may be 3-5 minutes long. A concert should not be longer than two hours. Also, timing a piece of music determines how long to work on it in rehearsal.

3. Reserve about 20-30 minutes of rehearsal for every minute.

For calculation's sake, I use decimal places instead of seconds. (Six seconds is .1 minute; so, 3 minutes and 8 seconds is about 3.1 minutes.) In my church choir, here are a list of anthems needing rehearsal for upcoming services:

PART THREE: Preparing for Rehearsal.

April 28 – Seek Ye the Lord – Peterson – 4.2 minutes

May 5 – Great is Thy Faithfulness – Hayes – 5.0 minutes

May 12 – Simple Thanksgiving – Martin – 3.6 minutes

May 19 – Sing and Shout – Harlan – 2.6 minutes

May 26 – If Ye Love Me – Tallis – 2.5 minutes

June 2 – All Creatures of Our God and King – Hayes – 3.7 minutes

June 9 – The Spirit of the Lord is Upon Me – Elgar – 7.1 minutes

June 16 - Come Dwell in Solomon's Walls – Stroope – 4.2 minutes

June 23 - Look at the World – Rutter – 4.8 minutes

4. **Identify which pieces are not new to the choir, as they require less rehearsal time than newer music.**

For our example, I marked the pieces performed in the past year with an asterisk. (*)

*April 28 – Seek Ye the Lord – Peterson – 4.2 minutes

*May 5 – Great is Thy Faithfulness – Hayes – 5.0 minutes

May 12 – Simple Thanksgiving – Martin – 3.6 minutes

Developing the Rehearsal Plan

May 19 – Sing and Shout – Harlan – 2.6 minutes
*May 26 – If Ye Love Me – Tallis – 2.5 minutes
June 2 – All Creatures of Our God and King –
  Hayes – 3.7 minutes
*June 9 – The Spirit of the Lord is Upon Me –
  Elgar – 7.1 minutes
*June 16 - Come Dwell in Solomon's Walls –
  Stroope – 4.2 minutes
*June 23 - Look at the World – Rutter – 4.8
  minutes

5. **Grade the music.**
- 1 is easy (or a pre-performed piece, sung relatively recently, that the choir knows well).
- 2 is moderate for the choir.
- 3 is difficult for the choir.

Each grade of difficulty represents 15 more minutes of rehearsal. (Grade 1 is 15 minutes per minute of the piece; Grade 2 is 30 minutes per minute of the piece; Grade 3 is 45 minutes per minute of the piece.) As the piece becomes more familiar, the grade level may go down.

*April 28 – Seek Ye the Lord – Peterson – 4.2
  minutes – grade 1
*May 5 – Great is Thy Faithfulness – Hayes – 5.0
  minutes – grade 1

PART THREE: Preparing for Rehearsal.

May 12 – Simple Thanksgiving – Martin – 3.6 minutes – grade 2

May 19 – Sing and Shout – Harlan – 2.6 minutes – grade 2

*May 26 – If Ye Love Me – Tallis – 2.5 minutes – grade 2

June 2 – All Creatures of Our God and King – Hayes – 3.7 minutes – grade 3

*June 9 – The Spirit of the Lord is Upon Me – Elgar – 7.1 minutes – grade 2

*June 16 - Come Dwell in Solomon's Walls – Stroope – 4.2 minutes – grade 1

*June 23 - Look at the World – Rutter – 4.8 minutes – grade 1

6. Create a spreadsheet of the pieces and the amount of rehearsal time needed.

I use a spreadsheet to determine the exact amount of time, calculating how much time I will need, and track how much time spent. This helps me balance out what needs to be done during each rehearsal. The example on the next page has the column "Time Needed" and "Total." "Warm-up" refers to additional warm-up time before the weekly service.

Developing the Rehearsal Plan

Date	Title	Composer	Time	Grade	Time Needed	24-Apr	1-May	8-May	15-May	22-May	29-May	Warm-up	Total
28-Apr	Seek Ye the Lord (already rehearsed)	Peterson	4.2	1	63	15						30	45
5-May	Great is Thy Faithfulness (already rehearsed)	Hayes	5	1	75	10	20					30	60
12-May	Simple Thanksgiving	Martin	3.6	2	108	15	15	20				30	80
19-May	Sing and Shout	Harlan	2.6	2	78	15	10	10	20			30	85
26-May	If Ye Love Me	Tallis	2.5	2	75	10	10	10	10	25		30	95
2-Jun	All Creatures of Our God and King	Hayes	3.7	2	111	20	15	15	20	15	20	30	135
9-Jun	The Spirit of the Lord is Upon Me	Elgar	7.1	1	107		15	15	15	10	20	30	105

PART THREE: Preparing for Rehearsal.

Date	Title	Composer	Time	Grade	Time Needed	24-Apr	1-May	8-May	15-May	22-May	29-May	Warm-up	Total
16-Jun	Come Dwell in Solomon's Walls	Stroope	4.2	1	63			10	10	10	15	30	75
23-Jun	Look at the World	Rutter	4.8	1	72			5	10	10	15	30	70
	TOTAL TIME:	SHOULD EQUAL 85 MINUTES OR LESS				85	85	85	85	70	70		

Total rehearsal time: 90 minutes.

7. Identify timing for each of the rehearsal dates.

For instance, on May 15, I will need to spend 20 minutes on "Sing and Shout," 10 minutes on "If Ye Love Me," and so on. I use that column to create a rehearsal plan, allocating the number of minutes from the spreadsheet.

Rehearsal for May 15		
Title	Composer	Rehearsal Time
Sing and Shout	Harlan	20

Developing the Rehearsal Plan

Rehearsal for May 15		
Title	Composer	Rehearsal Time
If Ye Love Me	Tallis	10
All Creatures of Our God and King	Hayes	20
The Spirit of the Lord is Upon Me	Elgar	15
Come Dwell in Solomon's Walls	Stroope	10
Look at the World	Rutter	10
TOTAL TIME:		**85**

8. *Create a rehearsal order that includes a 5-minute warm-up.*

Make sure to place the harder pieces toward the beginning of rehearsal.

Rehearsal Order for Wednesday:

7:30 - Warm-up
7:35 - Sing and Shout - Sunday's Anthem
7:55 - The Spirit of the Lord is Upon Me – Elgar
8:10 - All Creatures of our God and King – Hayes
8:30 - If Ye Love Me – Tallis

PART THREE: Preparing for Rehearsal.

8:40 - Come Dwell in Solomon's Walls – Stroope
8:50 - Look at the World – Rutter

Now I have a rehearsal order that has enough time for each piece. Before rehearsal, or in my preparation time before rehearsal begins, I identify the weakest sections of the piece, and prepare to rehearse them first by either having my music open to them or using a post-it note to mark it. Alternatively, I can write it in the rehearsal order:

Rehearsal Order for Wednesday:

7:30 - Warm-up
7:35 - Sing and Shout - Sunday's Anthem
7:55 - The Spirit of the Lord is Upon Me – review pg. 4-5
8:10 - All Creatures of our God and King - try this together – if still too difficult, review in sectionals.
8:30 - If Ye Love Me - try a cappella
8:40 - Come Dwell in Solomon's Walls – review all the way through
8:50 - Look at the World – review all the way through

9. **Once a plan has been developed, stick to it.**

Stay in the allotted time. This means keep the rehearsal focused on one section, if need be.

10. Rehearse using the whole-parts-whole method.

Whole-parts-whole means taking a section of a piece, rehearsing it, isolating the troubled section, fix the problems, and then rehearsing it within the larger section again. During the initial run-through, identify sections that need work, but try not to stop. Rehearse those sections separately that need additional work. These sections may be rehearsed forward to back, in reverse back to front, or in order of difficulty. Next, re-run the entire piece or section once the problems are fixed. When only a small amount of rehearsal time is available, rehearse only the most difficult section. If time is available, rehearse that most difficult spot, then reintegrate it into the larger work.

Getting ready for the concert

As concert time gets closer, the singers must adjust to performing the entire work non-stop. This is where sticky notes and whole-parts-whole becomes essential. In a once-per-week rehearsal, I start this process about four weeks from the concert. Have the choir sing the entire work, start to finish. Either use sticky notes placed on the

PART THREE: Preparing for Rehearsal.

troubled spots, or dog-ear pages during the choir's mini performance. After the entire major work is completed, acknowledge the choir's great accomplishment first before continuing, especially if it is the first time the choir has sung an entire multi-movement work from beginning to end. If time, go back and address some of the more glaring spots during that rehearsal. If not, make a list of the spots, and use them for the next rehearsal. Below is an example from a rehearsal order near concert time where we were performing Haydn's *Lord Nelson Mass*:

Haydn's Lord Nelson Mass "Miss List"

<u>Kyrie</u> –

Opening entrance – separate the top and bottom notes (no sliding, no "r"s)

Measure 32 – (after soprano first solo) – Sopranos on a high A

4 before B – entrance needs work.

<u>Quoniam</u>

Opening– Don't take this too fast yet

7 before B needs to be solidified (all entrances up to B) – and all entrances until C.

6 before the end – Sopranos need more help on entrance

<u>Et Incarnatus</u>

> A – solidify pitches
> <u>Et Resurrexit</u>
> Way too fast. Perhaps the look of panic in everyone's eyes was worth seeing
> Judicare entrance was not solid
> Measure 30 (Et in spiritum sanctum) and the other unison part are too loud; don't change dynamics
> E – solidify entrances
> <u>Benedictus</u>
> C – entrance not secure.
> <u>Agnus Dei/Dona Nobis</u>
> A – softer with correct notes.

Once this list is finished with all the errors worked out and corrected, run the entire work again. Continue this process in order to prepare the choir for standing and focusing for the extended length of time. Make sure the choir has standing and sitting cues, so they can fully practice the entire experience of performance.

Conclusion

By sticking to a well-timed rehearsal, the clock becomes the true leader, and the rehearsal becomes surprise-free. Wandering around aimlessly through the music becomes a habit best left in the past. We spend more time focused

PART THREE: Preparing for Rehearsal.

because the clock is our taskmaster. Emailing or distributing the rehearsal order before rehearsal says that we have work to do in our time together while fitting a tight schedule and creating a sense of urgency. Our accompanists know what to practice and our choir members know what they will miss if they must miss. Most importantly, having a rehearsal plan says to the choir that we directors care about the time that they spend with us.

PART FOUR:

The Rehearsal

Chapter 13

The Warm-Up

Stray thoughts always run rampant in my head. I'm constantly distracted by outside sound – the radio, the internet, a stray thought, a problem, a difficult situation, an innovation, or things that have nothing to do with music – fences, a plumbing problem, or new lights in the house. Life can sometimes be overwhelming. In rehearsal, the music must be number one. How do we unplug with these extra distractions tugging for our attention?

When I started including pausing in my choral rehearsals, things began to change.

Pause – the mental warm-up

"Pause" means meditation; the act of listening and receiving God's will. Before starting this practice, I was not growing as a conductor. I was not open to sound and the music in front of me. Also, I was *nervous* all the time. I lived in fear of rejection, of being laughed at, of being told that what I did was not good enough. The sense of fear was crippling and something I worked to overcome.

This nervousness comes from the ego – an aggrandized sense of self, which at times can be either over-inflated (as though I control lights, temperature, or rehearsal attendance in the middle of conducting!) or underinflated (where I am sure these choir members do not like me very much). My ego believes all musical experiences are up to me.

We must quit judging everything. Meditation exercises – secretly disguised as warm-up exercises – step us away from the ego. Our state of mind improves when we show up to do the work and allow God to be responsible for the result.

After all, *conducting is an act of internal acceptance.*

PART FOUR: The Rehearsal

These are the warm-up exercises we do as an ensemble each time we meet.

1. Breath

The breath is the most fundamental connection between us and our ensemble, the world around us, and the Earth.

- Stand tall, with head level and shoulders relaxed. The back should be arched, but not rigid.
- Breathe five times low and slowly, inhaling deliberately. Breathe as though the breath comes up through your feet.
- Using the breath, as though a beach toy, allow the breath to fill parts of the body, starting with the feet, the legs, the torso, the arms, and finally the head.
- While exhaling, think of expelling the self out into the universe. While inhaling, take in the energy that comes from the building in, the people nearby, and the plants that surround the rehearsal building.

2. Controlling the breath

- Breathing in, one more time, exhale with an "s" sound. Sustain the "s" as long as possible.
- Do this three times.

3. Awakening the body

The Warm-Up

- Move the head from side to side a total of ten times.
- Roll the shoulders back five times, and forward five times. Carefully watch the breathing, that it remains low in the chest and slow.
- Move the hips in a circular motion, five times in one direction, and then five times in another. Or, with older singers, move the hands upward to the left, center, and right.
- (This next exercise requires a lot of space and is especially suited for younger singers.) Stand with the legs spread apart at shoulder width. Drop the torso forward so that the arms dangle in front, like a marionette puppet. Now, fling the arms to the right, and allow the torso to follow the arms, in a motion that will finish with the arms and torso moving in a full circle. Allow the body to rest in the dangling marionette position before repeating a total of five times, followed by five times in the other direction. (This is a great exercise for waking up, too.)

4. *Find the center*

- Identify the core of the body, around the navel, and place the hands near that spot, palms facing toward the other hand, as though they are holding an imaginary ball.

PART FOUR: The Rehearsal

- Pretend that the hands, still holding the ball, bring the ball up to the sternum (chest bone), but still held out away from the body about 6 inches.
- Now, allow the hands to continue touching the ball (since the ball is invisible) but drop the ball down, parallel to the navel. When it reaches that point, the ball should bounce against an imaginary piece of wood, placed there to keep the ball from going any lower. In your hands, you will feel the stop and reverse direction. *Be careful not to pause at the bottom; allow the hands and the imaginary ball to bounce.* The hands should effortlessly move between the low point and the rise back toward the top. Try this at a variety of speeds and efforts – hard, soft, slow, fast.

Know where the feet are

You have studied the score. You have been tasked with running a rehearsal or performance. Other people, whether willingly or not, have put their faith in you. The Universe has put you in this spot, on this day, for exactly the right reason. Before continuing – whether that's continuing this exercise, starting a rehearsal, or conducting the Chicago Symphony – stay in this moment, not in judgement or in fear, but in acceptance. Like it or not, we are in the exact spot we are supposed to be in at this time. Going into a music-making activity by accepting rather than judging makes good leaders.

Commentary

I do these exercises before each rehearsal. Though I tend to come to rehearsal with a lot on my mind – doubts, distractions or any other things, the mental warm-up process quiets the mind and allows complete focus on the rehearsal.

The vocal warm-up process

The warm-up process takes about five minutes in rehearsal. It contains five parts: body, breath, vocalizing without rhythm, rhythmic vocalizing, and range extension. These are some suggested exercises to lead the choir from moments of non-rehearsal time into rehearsal time. When preparing the warm-up, typically only use one or two from each part.

1. Body
- Rolling the shoulders
- Twisting the torso
- Moving the head side-to-side
- Stretching up to the ceiling and to the left and right. (I use the terms north and south to stop confusion.)

PART FOUR: The Rehearsal

- (For younger choirs) stretching downward to the floor

2. Breath

- Breathe in through a straw
- Exhale on "s"
- Inhale into the shoulders, then to the chest, then to the hips, then fill the entire body with air
- Rhythm
- Have the choir repeat rhythmic exercises on explosive/fricative consonants such as "sh," "k," "ch". It is especially helpful to do this if there is a rhythm that needs to be addressed in the first piece.
- (For younger choirs) Use clapping along with fricative/explosive consonants to continue to engage the body.

3. Arhythmic vocalization

- A cappella singing is paramount at first: up and down the scale in thirds on a neutral vowel or with the voiced consonants "m" or "n," such as "mi, mi, mi..." or "ni, ne, na, no, nu"
- Unrhythmic vocalizing, focusing on moving the voice is best.
- Never go above an F above middle C/high C in the early exercises. Lower is better.

The Warm-Up

- Once you and the choir are sufficiently vocalized, move to the piano.

4. Rhythmic vocalization

- At the piano, use five-note scales in a rhythmic pattern that is relatively fast, or arpeggios that are fast. Vowels can be varied. Invent an accompaniment for these warm-ups. If not a great pianist, come up with a pattern that can be played in all keys. (I use I and V chords in a back and forth "boom-chick" pattern.)
- Graduate to a fast five-note or nine-note scale on any open vowel. These should be fast.

5. Range extension

- Using arpeggios, with an ah vowel at the top, and starting on the 5th of the scale, going up to the octave. I may go above the F, but not far. Sometimes I have the choir sing "I love(AH) to sing," or "I love(AH) the day."

The first minutes of rehearsal

Go straight into the first piece – in church choir, this means the anthem for Sunday morning – while their minds are most focused. Spend another 15-20 minutes preparing and perfecting this first piece. *Do not make announcements until after the first piece or at a break.* In church choir rehearsals, after the upcoming anthem, practice the most difficult anthem or section of an upcoming work, while everyone's mind is fresh. In community chorus, the hardest parts of the songs get rehearsed first.

I do this *every week*. It is so automatic that I never worry about planning the first half hour of rehearsal!

Conclusion

Truthfully, the warm-up is not for the choir, it is for the director. We focus to energize the singers' bodies, minds, and spirits in anticipation of singing. Yet, it is our own mental work, our own mental state, that needs the most preparation before rehearsal. Take the time to prepare – ignore the events of earlier or later in the day; focus on the music, because the reward is an hour or two of total connectivity to the ensemble, to the music, and to God.

Chapter 14

In the Rehearsal

Early in my career, my rehearsals were filled with pauses and down-time while I worked with sections one-on-one. First the sopranos, then the altos, and so on – always the same. It left people bored, so I peppered rehearsal with almost-funny jokes. Almost. Those choirs grinned and bore it. Others left.

I wanted to rehearse with the finesse that I had rarely seen in rehearsals. I wanted the choir regularly to experience that addictive time-consuming *flow* that comes from a well-paced rehearsal. Though everyone is different in their personalities, these techniques worked best for me, and hopefully you can adapt it for yourself.

How do we make the most out of a 60, 90, or even 180-minute rehearsal?

Previously, we talked about the rehearsal plan and creating a rehearsal order, but how do we execute that rehearsal in the most efficient and engaging way possible? In this chapter, we will look at some of the techniques to create an exciting rehearsal process that will keep the choir members coming back.

The warm-up

The beginning of the rehearsal sets the tone for the entire time. Of course, if possible, have a clock set up that you can see in the rehearsal space. In my rehearsal space we have two: one for me, one for the choir. They are synchronized.

Always start rehearsal on time. This is the most important part of rehearsal, as it says that what we do together is important. It says that we care about the choir members' time and energy that they spent coming to rehearsal.

The rehearsal

Once rehearsal has started, follow the plan that is lined out in your notes.

Excerpts that are easy for the choir

If the anthem or work is easy and relatively tonal, have the choir sing through an excerpt of it for no more than 2-3 minutes, unless it is so easy or so familiar, they can sight-read it or re-sing it. *The importance here is not that the music, diction, and phrasing are perfect; the purpose here is to familiarize the choir with the music if it is new, or re-acquaint them, if it has already been rehearsed.* Once the first run-through has occurred and there are no major problems, speak briefly about the phrasing, work on specific problems with the diction, and re-run the piece, if needed.

Sometimes, a review is all that is necessary. I call these pieces "gimme" pieces, which I use during especially difficult times of the year (our fundraiser, before our Christmas or Spring concerts, before beginning-of-the-year talent show). The purpose of these pieces is to save rehearsal time for the more difficult music.

Excerpts that are moderately difficult

Begin with the hardest part first, usually not the beginning, and move to the easier parts, then sing the selection all the way through. If the group has mastered the selection following the tough part, skip it. Move to the next difficult selection.

PART FOUR: The Rehearsal

Use sticky notes to mark where each of these difficult problems are and isolate them.

In the case of a missed entrance or a missed section, start by having the choir sing just the entrance, then ask the accompanist (or, with no accompanist, you) to play the measure before and see if the group can sing their first note. If not, have the choir hear the accompaniment right before, and hold their first note. Then after holding their first notes, sing the entire phrase. Repeat this selection without the hold.

Excerpts that are rather challenging

Divide the choir into *at least* two sections by voice part, and using two separate rooms, run through the challenging parts. I have learned when teaching a new piece, this creates variety and is much more efficient than working one part at a time. Even if the section leaders are volunteers who may not be as fast at teaching, new section leaders create a faster learning curve. Do not be afraid to switch up which sections rehearse together – the sopranos do not always *have* to rehearse with the altos. If the sopranos and tenors sing together often, maybe split up sectionals S-T, A-B.

During these sectionals, try not to run any rehearsals yourself – even if it means playing the piano for someone else. Choirs love variety and having a different section leader can go a long way to keeping the rehearsal interesting. In one choir, I asked four volunteers to run sectionals and I visited each sectional rehearsal, moving intermittently to hear them rehearsing. The choir grew before my eyes – all by themselves!

I often introduce new selections in a major work this way to cut down on the tedium of sight-reading in a group together. The very act of moving from one room to another also increases interest as the choir members are out of their chair and moving to another location or moving to another part of the room.

Rehearsing together

When time comes to rehearse together, there are some great techniques to increase excitement in the rehearsal: movement, mini performances, and circles.

1. Movement

Legendary choir conductor Robert Shaw believed that a common, exact pulse in the choir assisted in intonation as well as rhythmic energy and excitement. Inner pulse awareness is essential for choirs to reinforce the energy of each note, especially in long, sustained selections. Inner pulses are the smaller internal beats inside of a larger beat structure. In 4/4, for instance, the pulse would usually be the quarter note, and the inner

PART FOUR: The Rehearsal

pulse would be the eighth note. In 6/8, the pulse would be the dotted quarter note, and the inner pulse would also be the eighth note. To help create this rhythmic energy, the choir can use movement to reinforce that concept:

- Have the choir tap inner pulses such as eighth notes or sixteenth notes.
- Have the choir stomp or sway in unison.
- Count sing the excerpt while swaying to the beat or stomping to the beat.
- Have the choir clap out rhythms while half of the ensemble claps out inner pulses, then reverse.
- If the choir knows the melody well, have them put their music down, sway to the beat, and clap the rhythms, while singing *a cappella.* (This can be especially challenging, but especially satisfying!)

2. Mini performances

Having finished rehearsing the difficult selection, learned it in sectional rehearsals, and having an above-average comprehension of those pages, create a mini performance of them. Have the choir stand, start with either the beginning notes of that selection (or right before it as an introduction) and perform it. This gives a sense of accomplishment; they have made progress in that selection and have done well! At the end,

In the Rehearsal

congratulate them – even if it's not the best it could be! They already know it is not perfect yet; we do not need to tell them.

3. Circles

When I was teaching high school, this was one of the students' favorite techniques for learning. With volunteer choirs, they see it as a relaxation of some of the rigidity of sitting in sections – husbands stand next to wives and brothers next to sisters. In the community chorus, it works well if the group is small. Have the choir stand in a circle around the chairs of the rehearsal hall and create a mini performance. The singers should still stand next to other singers in their own section unless they feel strong enough in their own part to stand next to a singer of another part. Go through the excerpt. The singers will suddenly be able to hear themselves and hear other members with different parts, allowing them to see where their note fits in the entirety of the sonic tapestry.

Using the circle:
- A great seating arrangement for small choirs.
- If using this at the beginning of rehearsal, move the chairs before starting.

PART FOUR: The Rehearsal

- If using this as a mini performance, and the choir moves to this position, maintain it for a time as it is quite disruptive and anticlimactic if the choir moves back into sectional seating after having been able to see one another in the circle. You may use the circle technique to lead into the close of rehearsal.

The end of rehearsal

All good (and bad) rehearsals must come to an end, and yours should end with the same love and care as the beginning. The end of rehearsal should accomplish three things:
1. Remind singers that they are not alone as they leave.
2. Encourage singers about the work that they accomplished during the rehearsal time.
3. End with an expected, regular closing: a prayer, a song, or a common phrase.

Currently, at Cypress Creek, we end with a joys and concerns and a prayer time. Then I say, "Thank you for a great rehearsal." When I was in Brenham, we closed each rehearsal with the Lutkin *The Lord Bless You and Keep You*. At a church I worked at many years ago, we sang an original-composed hymn. Any of these are acceptable, and all create this space. Recently, as I have done the "joys and concerns" before prayer, I have found that the singers, encouraged to share individual thoughts and prayers, help me to identify who needs a helping hand, and who has wonderful news to share. It brings me closer to each of the singers. We end rehearsal with birthday night on the first Wednesday of the month, and "snack time," where we get to know each other better. In this way, we become more connected, and it helps our choirs grow.

After rehearsal

Once rehearsal is over, I sit down with the music either that night or the next day. Was there anything that did not work? Did I need a longer amount of time on a selection? Did my rehearsal plan fail in some way? Was I working too slowly or quickly?

The sticky notes come out and I quickly jot down areas on the score that need more help. Maybe a part needs to be run in sectionals, or entrances cleaned up. Maybe I need to work with a group on their diction, particularly if it's in a foreign language. Maybe the words themselves or the rhythms need to be addressed. I put these on sticky notes, attach them to the troubled areas, and leave them for other tasks, until it's time to put the next rehearsal order out, where I'll open them up,

PART FOUR: The Rehearsal

and once again my past-self reveals what my present-self needs to be doing.

Conclusion

Rehearsal is my favorite part of the music making process. We stretch ourselves, our singers, and our minds, ever reaching higher. We sometimes lead, sometimes follow, and always direct, allowing ourselves the ability to listen and accept the sounds that come to us – even if they are wrong. Then, our real work begins: to make those wrong sounds better.

PART FIVE:

The Rest of the Story

Chapter 15

What Else Do We Do?

Early in the morning of August 28, 2017, I received a text message. I was asleep when it came through.

"Joel, wake up! The Centrum's taking on water!"

Earlier that night I was on the phone with some friends when my power went out. Sitting there, in the dark, I heard the rainwater pouring down around my house. The usual sounds from outside masked by the hum of the refrigerator, buzz of the air conditioner, and whir of the ceiling

What Else Do We Do?

fans suddenly seemed much louder with the power out. The tree frogs creaked and the rain kept falling. It was the darkest I could have ever imagined my little house to ever be.

Inch after inch of rain fell.

I had lived in Houston much of my life and knew about strong storms, but this was different. It was biblical, it seemed. All I could do was try to get some sleep.

We sat in our house for 3 days until the rain let up. The grocery stores had closed, and by the time we could finally get back to the church, our performance hall had been inundated with several feet of water and a small number of fish. The Steinway was waterlogged, the robes were muddy, the smell was overpowering, and sheet music had been destroyed.

Yet, there was a hope in all of this. I was surrounded by people pitching in to move furniture and rinse the mud off. Love and support permeated the church as we threw out treasured items of forty years. We cleaned into the fall, through Christmas, into the next summer, and up to a year later. Still, we endured.

I remember sending an email to the ensembles to come help clean. Help they did, armed with bleach, large and small fans to dry music. We cleaned colleagues' offices, now ruined

PART FIVE: The Rest of the Story

and lost. People showed up from the community – renters of our facility, former church members, volunteers from the surrounding neighborhood all came. We stood together working to bring the music back to Northwest Houston.

At our Christmas concert, we had a sold-out crowd. Our music still matters.

Not just conducting

"What do you do?" I get this question from friends sometimes. In the past year, here is a list:
1. Made group travel arrangements.
2. Fixed items around the church using tools, cement, and wood.
3. Acted as an accountant for our 501(c)3.
4. Worked as a grant writer.
5. Prayed with people and visited choristers in the hospital.
6. Written notes and letters.
7. Spoken at funerals.
8. Acted as a host.
9. Written pieces of music and arranged music for different instruments.
10. Written and printed programs into small books.
11. Organized databases available on "the cloud."
12. Acted as a web administrator.

What Else Do We Do?

13. Given the board reports about our financial health.
14. Taped booths for the craft show.
15. Led health inspectors around to food vendors for our craft shows.
16. Prayed for others.
17. Written letters to the choir.
18. Cut into walls to add electrical outlets, hooks and run wires.
19. Chartered busses and arranged airline contracts.

These are just the ones I can think of off the top of my head. Being a conductor is just the beginning; it involves so much more than the music, but I try to never forget that the music is what brings us to doing these "other" tasks.

Conducting choirs, orchestras, bells, or any other ensemble is the best job in the world. Despite other activities that need attending, most of us, if asked why we conduct, it is because we couldn't imagine doing anything else. There are so many groups, yearning to have good conductors stand in front of them and believe in them. If you are reading this book, you are probably one of those people. If the heat is not working, if the rehearsal hall floods, if the sound system is ruined, if the pianist is sick, or if the soloist hurts himself, you

PART FIVE: *The Rest of the Story*

have the power to overcome all of these obstacles and make wonderful music happen.

May the peace of God be with you in those bad times; may He guide your baton and your heart; may He help you to make a difference in someone else's life through the power of music, and most of all, may the work that you do be an inspiration of others to "seek justice, love mercy, and walk humbly with our God."

Other tools for the choir director

1. A box of "regular" tools such as a tape measure, adjustable wrench, screw drivers, hammer, nails, screws, and a drill.
2. Work gloves – because we move equipment.
3. Measuring tape for clothes (dresses, robes, and tuxedos).
4. Basic knowledge of a sound system and stage lighting system.
5. A recording device for your choir of their concerts, particularly special church services or rehearsals.
6. A flashlight.
7. Matches for the assortment of candles that you will need to put out for concerts and various seasons and holidays (Christmas, Memorial Day, Holy Week).

8. For church directors, knowledge of the liturgical colors and when to use them.
9. A shareable folder with your choir library in it. This can be in a spreadsheet such as excel. I highly recommend having it online in a shared place like Google Drive, so both you and a few of your trusted assistants can access it.
10. Knowledge of anniversaries for different composers.
11. For church and temple musicians - regular contact with your senior pastor or rabbi for appropriate texts used in sermons.
12. A little tempered sass, to offset the people who tell you how to do your job better. Most people do this out of love or care.
13. A hobby away from the church. (I make fountains and work in my yard.)

For those whose calling is in the church

When I first started as a singer at a church in Fort Worth, I was not sure if this was the right path for me. I am a quirky Jewish man who works in a church and conducts choirs.

"How can you do that?" Some ask. "Isn't that against your religion?"

PART FIVE: The Rest of the Story

Some of us spend a great deal of our lives surrounded by Christianity. We learn to love the religion, the teachings, the liturgy, the colors, the acceptance, and the joy. And though my personal beliefs differ from those generally accepted in the church, I have found that we are all on a spiritual journey. Being a Jew in a Christian Church allows me a freedom from baggage that others have. I can ask the harder questions of, "Why do we have to do that?" since my childhood was not riddled with church camp, songs that *must* be sung, and rituals that *must* be obeyed. We fall into these traps not because the church tells us to do so, but because a beloved former pastor or elder or camp counselor said that we must do this. Being Jewish kept me out of a lot of the emotional struggles that may have been present had I grown up Christian.

I also have seen others from various sects of Christianity have similar responses. Those that grew up Catholic and working now in Protestant churches come to mind, or those that grew up in conservative denominations and now work in more liberal ones, or vice versa. Our job is to bring others close to God through music first.

In my church life, I found others just like me – I like to call us "Church groupies." We are the people who learn about, study, and discuss the spirit, worship God in churches on Sunday, but are

What Else Do We Do?

still Jewish. In the church world we are non-believers, yet we are welcome. There are several in my own church, and we all grow spiritually by helping others. I also learned that, as choir director my own religious beliefs do not matter – just my spiritual beliefs! I am not here to proselytize or convince others of my belief system or way of thinking. (Imagine what a mess that would be!) Instead, I lead others to enhance their *own* belief system by using the gifts I can bring into the rehearsal. Each person in his own way is drawn closer to God.

My real love is the community chorus. It has been the source of my best successes. Through music, we bring people united by a love of singing closer to God; it is a reminder that this same music has been bringing people together for centuries.

A few months ago, I went with several church members to the local synagogue. As a Jewish person, I explained some of the liturgy, the rituals, and what to expect. I intended to help others feel comfortable in such a strange environment – even though I, too was in an unfamiliar synagogue.

The result was startlingly revealing. The music was wrong. I knew the chants, and these were not correct! They were nothing like the ones I sang growing up. I became irritated. It just was not right.

Suddenly, I realized that I was making the same arguments and having the same discussions that I had heard in my church about the same thing! The music and the songs were unfamiliar; the prayers seemed wrong.

We all have this image, if we grew up in a religious body, that this is the way it is *supposed* to be. Children learn music and memorize much faster than adults, and so if the notes, the music, the songs, or the words are not *exactly* as they were when we were kids, we either rebel, explain, or learn to accommodate the differences. Our congregants have this same reaction. I did not have this experience growing up in church, and therefore can change things without my own personal reactions over new hymns or new ideas in the church or in the community chorus. Put me back in the synagogue and look out, my biases come forth vociferously.

One "controversy" that plagues church directors is Advent – the season right before Christmas from around Thanksgiving until December 24. Liturgy says that Advent is a time of waiting – celebrating the angel coming to tell Mary of the birth, the long journey from Nazareth to Bethlehem, and the arrival of the baby.

What Else Do We Do?

But for some, Advent means going to the store, hearing Christmas carols, watching *Miracle on 34th Street*, and miles and miles of *Jingle Bells*. (These carols are played intentionally in the store so we will buy more for our families and whomever else we think are important in our lives.)

It also means hearing Christmas carols in church. Advent was much more prominent until the department stores began playing Christmas music to motivate shoppers. Do we follow the liturgy? Do we capitulate to those singing "Joy to the World" on December 6th, even though Christmas has not come?

The sheepish among us would argue, "Can't we do both?" but music is a *temporal* art, and only one song can be performed at one time.

As the music director we make the choice. Many in our churches grew up with the nostalgia of Christmas carols played throughout December, and that by not doing so, it creates the same visceral reaction as this Jewish person not hearing the correct version of a chant. I have no great insights; except that this is something we must reckon with.

Conclusion

Develop a thick skin and a little wit, as people will challenge your musical choices. This does not necessarily indicate our choices are

PART FIVE: The Rest of the Story

wrong. It means that the music director must have the audacity to go up against these memories burned into many of our congregants' and audience's memories.

Chapter 16

If You Build It...

As I was learning to be a choir director, this statement *seemed* to be implied: pick good music, rehearse well, conduct well, and the singers will come. Just like that!

Summer comes, or spring break, Fourth of July, the Sunday after Christmas, the week after Easter, or the latest bout of sickness that has spread through every family in the church. (Originally, I wrote this paragraph in early 2019. As I rewrite it in 2020, I am amazed at the accuracy of this

PART FIVE: The Rest of the Story

statement.) I look up on Sunday morning and there are no tenors, four basses, one alto, and seventeen sopranos.

Volunteer choirs are for life but are not committed to a life sentence. Singers should have time off from singing. It is not our jobs to guilt them into being at church every Sunday or performing every concert. I know that in suburban Houston, my working choir members sometimes go out to visit parents or other family members out of town, leave with their kids, and occasionally just get tired. I never *ever* give them grief for this, but I do tell them I miss them.

Every week, I send a rehearsal order on Monday along with a note. Often, I write a small excerpt about the lesson coming this Sunday, some announcements, a list of upcoming special rehearsals or concerts, or anything else they need to have on their calendar. This way, the singers know what they will miss. I make sure their rehearsals are not a waste of time. We start rehearsal on time and end on time, every time. Basically, I respect the singers' time, and in return, they let me know if they cannot attend Wednesday or on Sunday. They know I will not waste their time, and know I expect the same from them.

If You Build It...

When they are missing

Yes, this has happened to me. No, it was not a disaster. Sometimes I know in advance and must change the anthem or performance, but *once the music is turned in to the bulletin, program or screen, I am stuck with it.* Here are some tips I have for when the choir is seriously unbalanced:
1. Have the loudest section sing a little quieter.
2. Divert singers who can read to sections that need more help (if you can spare them).
3. If no singers can read, see if the part can be left out, and then double all the parts at the organ/piano for extra security.
4. Have the pianist create the accompaniment to cover the missing parts.
5. Sing the missing part.

If all else fails, and you have picked a piece that uses all four parts in exposed solo selections, then change the piece to something they can do.

I like to have ready in the lineup pieces that don't need a lot of rehearsing, are easy, and can be pulled out and performed at a moment's notice. One of my early choirs knew *With a Voice of Singing* by Martin Shaw (1875-1958) very well – to the point of not needing music. It uses a loud organ part, and makes the choir, especially when small, sound large. I have found that these easy pieces vary with each choir. During the first year with each choir I notice which pieces they know well. At one church, John Carter's arrangement of *I Have Decided to Follow Jesus* was the favorite; at another, *Come Dwell in Solomon's Walls* by Z. Randall Stroope (b. 1953). One community chorus had *The Lord Bless You and Keep You* by Peter Christian Lutkin (1858-1934) while another used *The Spirit of the Lord is Upon Me* by Edward Elgar (1857-1934). Every chorus has one standby piece, and most choirs likely have several.

Letters to the Choir

Choirs like to know what is happening the next week, so that they know what they would miss if they neglect rehearsal. Here are some examples of what I send out on Mondays to my choir:

From August 23, 2017 – just days before the church was flooded:

> *Isaiah 40, the scripture for this week's sermon, reads "*[1]*Comfort, Comfort Ye My People." (Some know this as the text of the opening Tenor solo to* Messiah*)*
>
> *Comfort is a powerful thing – otherwise there wouldn't be peanut butter and chicken fried steak (or insert your own "comfort" food here – chocolate,*

marshmallows, asparagus, whatever makes you happy…) and in fact we all look for comfort in many things. Finding comfort in the daily trudge can be difficult at times, but we are reminded to be vigilant in this matter; that God gives us comfort.

Isaiah goes on: ⁹You who bring good news to Zion, go up on a high mountain. You who bring good news to Jerusalem, lift your voice with a shout, lift it up, do not be afraid: say to the towns of Judah, "Here is your God"

Why?? Because in between these texts – between telling of comfort, and the good news – between these texts set so famously by Handel, comes a darker text, set famously by Johannes Brahms (1833-1897) in the second movement of his Requiem:
⁶All people are like grass, and all human faithfulness is like the flowers of the field.

PART FIVE: The Rest of the Story

[7]The grass withers and the flowers fall, because the breath of the Lord blows on them.

Ouch. A harsh juxtaposition, indeed. With words like that, we need a little comfort.

Another letter – my opening letter to the choir after I had just accepted my current position:

Dear Choir,

First of all, thank you, thank you, thank you, for asking me to come and work with you. I know you had many choices, and I am humbled and honored to be working with you soon, and am literally counting the days until our first rehearsal together.
Now, many of you are wondering what we are going to be doing for Christmas. This week, I will be meeting with various people to begin the planning, and, we should be ready to start on music very, very soon, after I have all of the information about how your Christmas concerts were

If You Build It…

structured, so that I can continue the wonderful tradition that has been at CCCC for many years.

My thoughts about rehearsal - at this point, looking at it from many miles away - is to keep rehearsals from 7:30-9, with equal time being devoted to anthems and music for the service (7:30-8:15) and community chorus (8:15-9). I would like to, at this point, have two Saturday rehearsals on November 7 and November 14, (Dickens weekend is November 20-21) specifically for the Christmas concert. The time of these rehearsals most likely will be 10AM-12Noon, but again, I'll have more information about possible conflicts with those times later this week. By our first rehearsal together on September 23, these dates and times will be clearly defined for you.

Finally, I think you should know that I will be working with Bruce, Ann, Dennis and Clara on making this transition as smooth as possible for you. I know that changing choir

PART FIVE: The Rest of the Story

directors is probably one of the most difficult events that a chorister can face. I have a great deal of faith in each of you, after seeing the work you did a few weeks ago, about your enthusiasm for singing and the community that we will continue to grow week after week. I await many days of laughter, tears, music-making, coffee, dessert, lunches, and walking through the spiritual journey that is music-making together with you and will do my best to support each of you as your new director. I can never replace Dennis or Clara, but I hope you know that I share your love of choral music, as they do, and will put all my love and artistry that I have towards giving you a connection of the divine through our voices.

If there is anything you would like to talk about, I am only a short phone call away. Again, I look forward to serving as your director soon. I hope to update you in about a week on Christmas and our upcoming events.

If You Build It...

Blessings, and all my very best,
Joel

I write letters and send them before each rehearsal. Sometimes they discuss a recent musical experience, or about a piece of music to be performed. Sometimes I refer to a passage on singing or a reading of scripture, along with commentary. I always write. I do it every Monday morning, and it works.

Setting Expectations

I had the privilege of watching a college conductor direct a massed choir of students from different schools, and, in a short number of days, create an excellent performance. Her approach to rehearsal was exciting and dynamic, and her rehearsal technique was flawless. The way she impressed me the most happened at the very beginning of the first rehearsal.

It happened in the first five minutes. The students had been assembled and introduced to her. She looked at them, head turning to the left, and then to the right sizing up the enormous group in front of her.

She then set up her expectations. At her first breath she said, "Our time together is precious, and

PART FIVE: The Rest of the Story

I want to give you 100 percent. I hope that you'll do the same for me. So this is what I would like…"

She then named off rehearsal behaviors: being on time, not talking to one's neighbor, and not using the restroom in the middle of rehearsal. In the few days that followed, the students were focused and intent. They remained focused; not talking to one another or going to the restroom during rehearsal. She used their time wisely, and they gave her their best work, just like she asked at the beginning.

I went home to my college choir and that afternoon I tried it. I told them how precious our time was, and that I would give them my best, and I asked them to do the same. I asked them to not use the restroom during class, to refrain from talking to one another, and to give me their best, and I would do the same. I do this now after every Summer hiatus, after every Christmas break, and after every long pause in rehearsals. I set up my expectations, in a loving, positive way, and it works. I never actually met the conductor that weekend, but her lesson was profound: give the expectations, and they will be received.

Maybe instead of "If you build it, they will come," it should be "If you expect it, it will happen."

Conclusion

Today, a quarantine is in full swing, "social distancing" is the norm, and I have not seen my choir in a month, with more months possibly on the way. I always subscribed to the notion that rehearsal should happen no matter what. I rehearsed right before Hurricane Harvey inundated our church and community center. I have rehearsed during tornado warnings and snowstorms. Rehearsal is so important to me I will not cancel it for anything.

Then the COVID quarantine happened.

I am awestruck at how our entire world has come to a standstill; and even more amazed at how much I rushed around from one thing to the next, always busy. This time has enabled me to do more practicing at the piano, more praying, more long walks with my husband through the neighborhood, and more time with friends and former students on the phone or via email.

Frequently choir members ask me why we cannot rehearse through the technologies that exist. I tell them about the half-second lag, and that while in speech this is acceptable, in song it is not. I am still amazed that making music is so special that it requires us to be together.

"But I saw a group on the internet rehearsing together," some say.

PART FIVE: The Rest of the Story

I then explain that each person recorded his or her part separately, and then they are edited together, much in the same way as I edited a psalm response so that I could play the organ, stand at a podium and sing all at the same time. I realize, in moments like this, just how special our choral art is. What we do as choral musicians depends on light and proximity. Simply put, no matter what the technology, we cannot make music unless we are in line of sight with each other.

I am hopeful that when this quarantine is over, we realize that music is even more special than we thought.

Chapter 17

Coda

There are some studies that suggest our profession is getting smaller. In fact, we live in a world where everyone has a voice now. We exist in a place where all is available for everyone to see. More than ever, as a society we believe in the unworthy; the unlovable; the unusable. People, good people, are cast off every day as fodder; throwaways that have nothing left to contribute.

It is, frankly, disheartening.

PART FIVE: The Rest of the Story

In our industry – in our musical profession – many people get lambasted on the internet. On YouTube I watched a video of a piece I was preparing about a year ago, performed by a nearby church choir. Multiple people pressed the "dislike" button and shared in the comments how the performance was not correct. It was either not fast enough or articulate enough or authentic enough or some other thing. I thought to myself "YOU put a group of volunteers together and YOU conduct that piece, and we'll see how it goes!"

We live in a society of the unredeemable, the inexcusable, and the unacceptable. In this place, there are a great deal of clamoring voices that gladly give their opinions. The number of armchair conductors is amazing! Unfortunately, this is not new.

One of the greatest musical experiences I ever had was to sing Benjamin Britten's *War Requiem* with the New York Philharmonic under Kurt Masur. Masur worked us hard. He stretched his orchestra to their potential, pushing players, soloists, and sub-conductors. We sang our best for him because he would not have it any other way.

On the second night's performance in Avery-Fischer Hall, an older man sat down in the front-center section. I could see him easily from my vantage point in the choir. He had a long white beard and was vaguely reminiscent of Santa Claus. As the opening strings played the foreboding half-step, before the first clang of the tubular bells, Santa Claus, with a smug look, laid his *War Requiem* score on his lap and opened to the first page. The smirk on his face was not one of remembrance or curiosity; it was a judgement call to see if we (the choir and orchestra) would sing the notes correctly; to play effortlessly.

No good work is effortless, and no concert or service ever comes across perfectly. As a flawed human being, sometimes I can become obsessed with the errors. The tenors missed their note, or the sopranos were under pitch or the altos just did not sing.

Even worse is where I make an error. These problems are especially poignant because they are mine. They are big errors. Santa Claus – or someone like him – will always be with us watching.

When I was in the sixth grade, I loved choir and at the last concert I was asked to come forward for an award. As the audience clapped, I walked to the edge of the risers. Looking down from my top-row vantage point (I was tall for a sixth grader) I knew that instead of going through three rows of risers with other kids it would be much easier just

PART FIVE: The Rest of the Story

to jump down. The audience was clapping! I needed to hurry!

As soon as my sixth grade oddly large feet left the riser, I knew I had made a mistake.

My elegant glide to the bottom was interrupted when the curtain snared my foot and I flipped sideways. I fell face down into the institutional, greasy, green stage carpet. The other boys laughed. I tried to downplay it and maintain my "cool" exterior.

The next day in class was the worst. We watched the video of the concert that day and when we got to the spot where I fell, the class rewound the VCR, watching it over, and over, and over, and over. They laughed every time.

Much like falling in front of my sixth-grade buddies, sometimes I will try to watch in my mind a mistake I made over, and over, and over, and over again. Choral directing has an inherent ego deflating experience, especially when we mess up. How often do we assassinate someone else's character and inflate our own position by replaying that tape over and over, commenting on YouTube or quietly judging our colleagues?

We stand in front of a group of people every week and gesture for them as though we possess control over them, but the results are out of our hands! If, in front of that choir, we find people that

Coda

believe in us, we should stay close to them. When choirs get tough, act out, sing poorly, or cannot get their part, focus on the good. Though we may be their best choral director, or one of the worst, today they each chose to come and sing for us. That person could have been sleeping in, playing with their kids, coming home from work, or participating in a totally different hobby offered by countless groups. Instead, they chose to spend their time with us!

Seeing my choir each week is my best affirmation; I hope it is yours, too.

As you continue your musical journey, know that many of us had to learn by experiencing difficult times, and are still amazed at what wonderful sounds can come from our choirs with just a little hard work and practice.

As we close our time together, I leave you with this thought:

The choir is in your hands.
Do your best.
Be your best.
Even if you think it's not enough.
For conducting is an act of internal acceptance.
The music is what reaches others, not you.
Allow yourself to be a conduit for the music that will eventually reach them.
And keep coming back to rehearsal.

Further Reading

Brock McElheran. *Conducting Technique for Beginners and Professionals*, third edition. Oxford University Press, 2004.

Elizabeth A.H. Green and Mark Gibson. *The Modern Conductor*, seventh edition. Pearson, 2004.

Joseph Labuta. *Basic Conducting Techniques*, seventh edition. Routledge, 2017.

Gunther Schuller. *The Compleat Conductor*. Oxford University Press, 1988.

Stacy Horn. *Imperfect Harmony: Finding Happiness Singing With Others*. Algonquin Books: 2013.

Acknowledgements

Over the past several years, this book has slowly taken shape after different ideas, edits and comments helped turn it into what it is today, and many people have had a part in making it happen. Many people have given me insight either through their own experience, through sharing their wisdom with me, or by walking with me.

Thank you to…

My mom Debbie, dad Carl, and step-dad Gilbert, for teaching me to love life, wherever it takes me.

My sister and brother-in-law, Heather and Paul, who always stood in my corner through the thick and the thin.

I'm a Choir Director??!

The many teachers I had along the way who taught me to love music, writing, and conducting. There are too many to mention, and some have since passed on to the Great Rehearsal.

Mary Hupman, Julie Callaway and Emily Butner-Burroughs, who encouraged me to write down the ideas presented in my "changing meters in conducting" workshop. Thank you for encouraging me to restart this project after I had put it on the back burner for so many years.

Cindy Johnson and Darryl Fleishman, who suggested coming out to Smithville to spend time writing and spending time with them. This way I could take time off and enjoy my evenings after writing all day.

Pastor Bruce Frogge for suggesting targeting this book at newer volunteer choir directors.

Paula and John Gembala, for being my friends from the first time we met.

Linda and Randy Patterson – my cheering supporters through the transition out of academia and into church.

Gavin and Sharon Craig who welcomed me into Spring and have been great supporters, and for Gavin, who read this book cover-to-cover.

The choirs and handbell choirs of Cypress Creek Christian Church – you have been invaluable in allowing me to explore the possibilities of this

Acknowledgements

book and the freedom to make it happen, and the congregation which week-after-week shows up to worship God and come to our concerts.

My wonderful editor, Michelle Faught, who read and commented on each iteration of this book and kept encouraging me and asking when the next draft will be ready.

Debbie Rawlins, who made sure the words and the intention all made sense in this book, offering also to read multiple versions over and over and not judging me. (I am happy to continue fixing your plumbing or electrical problems.)

Tiana Pickle, a wonderful friend who offered on her own to read and edit this book and had me remove almost half – almost – of the dashes.

Yung Chiu Wang, for walking together side-by-side as a friend in our careers over many years.

Anne and Bobby Guess, for stopping me from choosing a different career along the way.

Ann Frohbieter, a friend, support, colleague, and a person whom I aspire to be more like.

Pastor Jon Stouffer, one of my staunchest supporters, who encouraged me to follow my heart and work with volunteer choirs full-time.

My friends and colleagues of the Association of Disciples Musicians.

Michael, my steadfast companion and husband. You helped create the life and home I always dreamed of and never knew I could have. For listening when I was upset, for making me laugh, and not taking me too seriously. For allowing me into your life and being a part of mine. I am fortunate and blessed to have you in this journey.

My God, who never abandoned me in the good days and in the bad ones. May these words on these pages be acceptable in your sight, my rock and my redeemer.

About the Author

Dr. Joel Plaag is choir director and Director of Traditional Worship at Cypress Creek Christian Church in Spring, Texas, a suburb of Houston, where he directs the chancel, bell, and children's choirs and directs the Cypress Creek Community Chorale. He has held the ranks of instructor, assistant professor, and associate professor at colleges in Texas and Arkansas. Churches he has served at include First United Methodist Church of Brenham, Holy Cross Lutheran Church of Houston, and First Christian Church of Grand Prairie, as well as a staff singer at churches and synagogues including Congregation Beth-El of Fort Worth, Emmanuel of Livingston, NJ, and Westcliff United Methodist of Fort Worth. He holds degrees from Texas Christian University

I'm a Choir Director??!

(B.Mus.Ed.), Westminster Choir College of Rider University (M.Mus.), and the University of Houston (D.M.A.). Major professors include Ronald Shirey, Ruth Whitlock, Joseph Flummerfelt, and Charles Hausmann. He has also studied orchestral conducting with Robert Gutter and Ovidiu Bãlan. Dr. Plaag's major research area is conducting pedagogy, and he can often be found teaching workshops on directing choirs. He is married to Michael Rebner and together they have two dogs, Teddy and Freckles.

www.ingramcontent.com/pod-product-compliance
Lightning Source LLC
Chambersburg PA
CBHW021949290426
44108CB00012B/1000

9780578678771